BERGH

FAMOUS IRISH SONGS
A. WOODS/S. KÖHL

FAMOUS IRISH SONGS

With the lyrics, the score and guitar support

Collected by
Armin Woods / Stefan Köhl

BERGH

BERGH PUBLISHING, Inc.
New York

ISBN 0-930267-17-6
© BERGH PUBLISHING, Inc., 1989
275 Fifth Avenue
New York, N.Y. 10001
Tel. (212) 686-8551
FAX (212) 779-2290
Sales & Distribution:
The Talman Company, Inc.
150 Fifth Avenue
New York, N.Y. 10011
Tel. (212) 620-3182
FAX (212) 627-4682

Photograph of Irish House and Landscape
by Edition Schönemund, Bonn, West Germany
Editor and Translator of Forword and Background Notes:
Nancy Dargel.
Printed in Sweden by
Vänersborgs Offset AB
Vänersborg 1990

Contents

6

Foreword

The seventy well-known Irish songs in this book were chosen by two musicians *for the sake of the singing.* Armin Woods and Stefan Köhl are members of a Rock Group in Munich. Köhl is a co-founder of the Munich Music School called *Ohrwurm* ("the earwig"). Köhl was born January 9, 1957 and Woods November 27, 1960. Woods comes of Irish stock on his father's side and a musical family on his mother's. His musical education started with a piano when he was five and went on to a thorough grounding in classical music. He then found his own way to Modern music and in recent years has become increasingly involved in Rock, West Coast, New Wave, etc. Köhl likewise first learnt to play the piano and then started the guitar in his thirteenth year. Later, he studied under H.G.Rausch and L.Henneberger, who were his teachers for Classical and Jazz guitar-music in Munich.

Background notes on Irish Folk Songs and Music

It is characteristic of Folk Music that its history should be hard to look into or write down. How much simpler things are when we have to do with the works described as classical! Think of the well-documented Firts Performance of Händel's *Messiah* — in Dublin, in 1742, with an Irish choir and an Irish orchestra! He had written it all, before anyone heard it, and there was the date!

Folk music goes from mouth to mouth and from ear to ear. The poeple who play it and sing it are not usually professionals; they heard it from somebody else; it was passed on. One song may have many variations, many different versions, and may indeed live on through perpetual change. Neither the tune nor the words remain steady from one generation to the next. Verses may be added or deleted according to the singer's mood. The tune may change to suit his personal register or the instrument he plays.

Many Irish songs may well have been Celtic in origin, but one can say for sure that the way the Celts sang them is not the way they are sung today. Neither did the words and the tune form an indivisble entity in earlier times. In the Middle Ages it was quite normal to use the same tune for a canticle in church in the morning and a drinking song in the tavern at sundown. As late as Tudor times, to take something still familiar to us, did not the tune of an older Christmas carol become that of *Greensleeves* — a Hit for far more than one London season and back with us again (with a new lyric!) in this present Twentieth Century?

It was not until the middle of the Eighteenth Century that anyone thought of collecting Folk Songs — usually Ballads, to begin with. Romanticism in the following Century then brought a surge of interest in the past, in our forefathers and there various forms of expression. Perhaps they had pursued nobler ideals, had known a better world. . .?

At lenght the *Twentieth* Century saw an authentic boom in Irish Folk Music publications.

This did not mean any kind of break in the oral tradition. The ''old'' songs — some born i Celtic times, some in 1920 — have continued to develop and evolve. Almost all of them have kept place with the development of the musical instruments; many of them could not have come into being at all without the highly developed instruments of today. Not that there was any scarcity of musical instruments in Celtic Ireland, only they were differnt from the ones we use now.

The best-known traditional Irish musical instrument is the *Harp.* Not one of the ancient Harp melodies has survived. The old method of playing, plucking the strings with one's fingernails, died out in the *XVIIIth.* century. Contemporary Irish singers, accompanying themselves with the harp, frequently use tunes originally written for the piano, and it may sound very nice indeed, but the tunes are not very old.

Nevertheless, Ireland may well have some claim to being the richest of the West-European countries in respect of genuine Folk Music. The most popular instruments remain the various kinds of Pipes, the Fiddle, the Flute, the Penny Whistle, the Concertina and the Harmonica or Mouth-Organ. Fifty years ago even the smallest village would have had at least one musician to play at festivities and at all kinds of community-singing events, as well as the numerous Folk Music Festivals (fleadh cheoil), that take place every year.

It would hardly be exaggerated to say that every household had its musician. Their numbers have dropped considerably since the advent of Radio and Television, although there has been no corresponding drop in people's interest in Folk Music, in fact quite the opposite. Listeners' Statistics show larger numbers for *Radio and Telefis Eireann's* music programs than for any other individual feature. The Irish still prefer singing and dancing to the old tunes rather than the new ones.

One could not enumerate a tenth part of the delightful songs and tunes that are still sung nowadays. There are collections of them and books about them. The best are perhaps two books with the same title: *Ancient Music of Ireland,* one by Petrie and the other by P.W. Joyce, together with the latter's *Old Irish Folk Music and Songs;* all three books are hard to come by nowadays. The *Irish Folk Commission* has a huge collection of material, much of which has already been published, although the greater part has not appeared yet. Many of the best-known songs are also dances. Most of these are now only sung, but it is essential to dance to them if one is to grasp their vitality and the sense of their repetitions. Many songs have served a political purpose since the days of *Lilliburlero and Shan Van Vocht.* Songs like *The Rising of the Moon* are a whole period in themselves; generations, clinging to their ideals, have sought comfort in them in troubled times.

Contemporary Ireland has an abundance of Music Groups, almost in every village. Some are only known in Ireland, others have international repute. The two most famous are probably *The Clancy Brothers and Tommy Makin* and *The Dubliners.* The Clancy Brothers come from County Tipperary; Tommy Makin, who sings with them, comes from Armagh. The Group has perfomerd to enthusiastic audiences in almost every town in the Republic as well as City Hall, Belfast. Perhaps that is a good sign. In the Arts as in Sports, Ireland ignores the borderline; the applause for Michael McLiammoir is the same in Belfast and Dublin. Indeed, the Clancy Brothers may owe some part of their success to a kind of provocation, to their disregard for the political boundary.

To be sure, Ireland lies on the edge of the Continent. There are historic reasons, as well as economic and social ones, for the fact that Ireland is poor in symphonic music and has produces no really outstanding composer of orchestral music. The creative power of the land lives on unbroken in her Folk Music, which has been able to preserve its innate vitality through the centuries. It would not be so surprising if the next few decades brought an extensive reanimation of musical productivity to the Green Isle. There are signs and pointers already now.

Harmonies

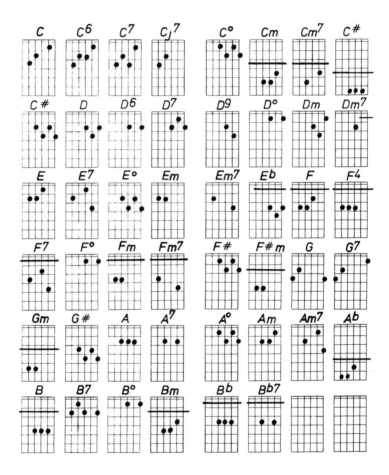

Harmonies

In many cases a useful *harmony* is I−IV−V−I. For instance, in B^b major: $B^b−E^b−F^7−B^b$, with the corresponding minor key Gm. If you want to play it in another key, say F major, the chords will be I−IV−V−I $\longrightarrow$ F−B^b−C^7−F. The minor key becomes tone major.

Another useful harmony is II−V−I. In C major: Dm−G^7−C. This can be put into another key in the same way — for instance into G major: Am−D^7−G.

Often enough there will be a diminished chord (D^o). A diminished chord is made up of a number of minor thirds and can be interchangeable. A D^o chord is at the same time an F^o, A^{bo}, B^o.

Drinking Songs

The Cruiskeen Lawn

Let the far-mer praise his grounds, Let the sportsman praise his

hounds, The shep-herd his sweet scen-ted lawn, But I, more blest

than they, Spend each hap-py night and day   with my charm-ing

lit ⁻tle cruis-keen lawn, lawn, lawn, With my charm-ing lit-tle

cruis-keen lawn.   Gra-ma-chree cruis-keen Gra-ma-chree cruis-

keen char-ming lit–tle cruis-keen lawn, lawn, lawn, Oh my

charm-ing lit ⁻tle cruis-keen lawn.

The Cruiskeen Lawn

1. Let the farmer praise his grounds,
   Let the sportsman praise his hounds,
   The shepherd his sweet scented lawn,
   But I, more blest than they,
   Spend each happy night and day
   With my charming little cruiskeen lawn, lawn, lawn,
   With my charming little cruiskeen lawn.
Chorus
   Gramachree cruiskeen Gramachree cruiskeen
   Charming little cruiskeen lawn, lawn, lawn,
   Oh my charming little cruiskeen lawn.

2. Immortal and divine, Great Bacchus, God of wine,
   Create me by adoption thy son,
   In hopes that you'll comply that my glass will ne'er run dry,
   Nor my smiling little Cruiskeen lawn lawn lawn.
   Nor my smiling little Cruiskeen lawn.
Chorus

3. And when grim death appears, after few but happy years,
   And tells me my glass it is run,
   I'll say, Begone, you slave, for great Bacchus gives us leave
   To drink another Cruiskeen lawn lawn lawn
   To drink another Cruiskeen lawn.
Chorus

4. Then fill your glasses high, lets not part with lips adry,
   Tho' the lark now proclaims it is dawn,
   And since we can't remain, may we shortly meet again,
   To fill another Cruiskeen lawn lawn lawn
   To fill another Cruiskeen lawn.
Chorus

The Moonshiner

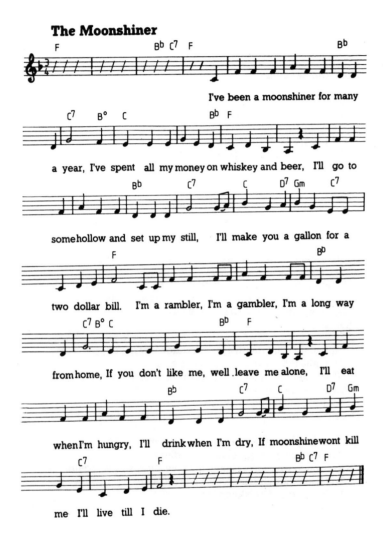

I've been a moonshiner for many a year, I've spent all my money on whiskey and beer, I'll go to some hollow and set up my still, I'll make you a gallon for a two dollar bill. I'm a rambler, I'm a gambler, I'm a long way from home, If you don't like me, well .leave me alone, I'll eat when I'm hungry, I'll drink when I'm dry, If moonshine wont kill me I'll live till I die.

The Moonshiner

1. I've been a moonshiner for many a year,
   I've spent all my money on whiskey and beer,
   I'll go to some hollow and set up my still,
   I'll make you a gallon for a two dollar bill.

Chorus
   I'm a rambler, I'm a gambler, I'm a long way from home,
   If you don't like me, well leave me alone,
   I'll eat when I'm hungry, I'll drink when I'm dry,
   If moonshine won't kill me I'll live till I die.

2. I'll got to some hollow in this counterie,
   Ten gallons of wash I can go on the spree,
   No woman to follow and the world is all mine,
   I love none so well as I love the moonshine.

Chorus

3. Moonshine, dear moonshine, oh! how I love thee,
   You kill'd my poor father, but dare you try me,
   Bless all moonshiners and bless all moonshine,
   Its breath smells as sweet as the dew on the vine.

Chorus

4. I'll have moonshine for Liza and moonshine for May,
   Moonshine for Lu and she'll sing all the day,
   Moonshine for my breakfast, moonshine for my tea,
   Moonshine, my hearties, it's moonshine for me.

Chorus

Ballads

Barney Brallaghan's Courtship

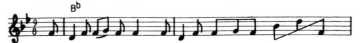

'Twas on a wind-y night, at two o-clock in the morn-ing An

I-rish lad so tight, All wind and weath-er scorn-ing, At

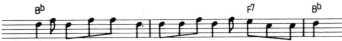

Ju-dy Cal-lagh-an's gate sit-ing up-on the pal-ing, His love

tale did re-late and this was part of his wail-ing. On-ly say

You'll have Mis-ter Bral-la-ghan Don't say may Charm-ing Ju-dy

Cal-la-ghan.

Barney Brallghan's Courtship

1. 'Twas on a windy night,
   At two o'clock in the morning
   An Irish lad so tight,
   All wind and weather scorning,
   At Judy Callaghan's gate

Siting upon the paling,
His love tale did relate
And this was part of his wailing.
Chorus
Only say you'll have Mister Brallaghan
Don't say may charming Judy Callaghan.

2. Ah list to what I say,
Charms you've got like Venus,
Own your love you may,
There's only a wall between us
You lie fast asleep
Snug in bed and snoring.
Round the house I creep
Your hard heart imploring.
Chorus ...

3. I've got an old Tom Cat,
Thro' one eye he's staring,
I've got a Sunday hat,
Little the worse for wearing
I've got some gooseberry wine
The trees had got no riper on,
I've got a fiddle fine,
Which only wants a piper on.
Chorus ...

4. I've got an acre of ground,
I've got it set with pratees,
I've got a baccy a pound
I've got some tea, for the ladies,
I've got the ring to wed
Some whiskey to make us gaily,
A mattress, feather bed,
And a handsome new shillelah.
Chorus ...

5. You've got a charming eye,
    You've got some spelling, and reading,
    You've got, and so have I,
    A taste for genteel breeding,
    You're rich, and fair, and young,
    As everybody's knowing,
    You've got a decent tongue,
    Whene'er it's set agoing.
Chorus ...

6. For a wife till death,
    I am willing to take ye,
    But och, I waste my breath,
    I'm hoarse in trying to wake ye,
    'Tis just beginning to rain,
    So I'll get under cover,
    I'll come tomorrow again,
    And be your constant lover.
Chorus ...

Cockles And Mussels

In Dublin's fair Ci-ty Where the girls are so pret-ty, I first

set my eyes on sweet Mol-ly Ma-lone: As she wheel'd her wheel

bar-row, Thro' streets broad and nar-row, Cry-ing "Cock-les and

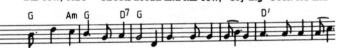

Mus-sels a-live a-live o! A-live, a-live o! A-live, a-live o!

Cry-ing Cock-les and Mus-sels a-live, a-live o!"

Cockles And Mussels

1. In Dublin's fair City
   Where the girls are so pretty,
   I first set my eyes on sweet Molly Malone.
   As she wheel'd her wheel barrow,
   Thro' streets broad and narrow,
   Crying "Cockles and Mussels alive alive o!"
Chorus
   "Alive, alive o! Alive, alive o!
   Crying Cockles and Mussels alive, alive o!"
   As everybody's knowing,
   You've got a decent tongue,
   Whene'er it's set agoing.
Chorus ...

Dan O'Hara

Sure it's poor I am today for

God gave and took a-way And He left without a home poor Dan O'

Ha-ra. With these matches in my hand in the frost and snow I

stand, So it's here I am today your broken hearted. A - chus-la

geal mo chree, Won't you buy a box from me And you'll have the

prayers of Dan from Con-ne-ma-ra, I'll sell them cheap and low,

Buy a box before you go From the poor old broken farmer Dan O'

$Fm^7 Bb^7 Eb$

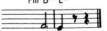

Ha-ra.

Dan O'Hara

1. Sure it's poor I am today for God gave and took away
   And He left without a home poor Dan O'Hara.
   With these matches in my hand in the frost and snow I stand,
   So it's here I am today your broken hearted.
Chorus
   Achuslageal mo chree, Won't you buy a box from me
   And you'll have the prayers of Dan from Connemara,
   I'll sell them cheap and low,
   Buy a box before you go
   From the poor old broken farmer Dan O'Hara.

2. In the year of sixty four I had acres by the score
   And the grandest land you ever ran a plough through.
   But the landlord came you know and he laid our old home low,
   So it's here I am today your brokenhearted.
Chorus ...

3. For twenty years or more did misfortune cross our door.
   And my poor old wife and I were sadly parted.
   We were scattered far and wide and our children starved and
   died.
   So it's here I am today you brokenhearted.
Chorus ...

4. Tho' in frost and snow I stand sure the shadow of God's hand.
   It lies warm about the brow of Dan O'Hara.
   And soon with God above I will meet the ones I love,
   And I'll find the joys I lost in Connemara.
Chorus ...

Has Sorrow Thy Young Days Shaded

Has sorrow thy young days shad-ed, As clouds o'er the morning

fleet? Too fast have those young days fad-ed, That e-ven in

sorrow were sweet. Does time, with his cold wing with-er, Each

feeling that once was dear? Then child of mis-for-tune come

hi- ther, I'll weep with thee tear for tear.

Has Sorrow Thy Young Days Shaded

1. Has sorrow thy young days shaded,
   As clouds o'er the morning fleet?
   Too fast have those young days faded,
   That even in sorrow were sweet.
   Does time, with his cold wing wither,
   Each feeling that once was dear?
   Then child of misfortune come hither,
   I'll weep with thee, tear for tear.

2. Has hope, like the bird in the story,
   That flitted from tree to tree,
   With the Talisman's glittering glory,
   Has hope been that bird to thee?
   On branch after branch alighting,
   The gem did she still display,
   And when nearest and most inviting,
   Then waft the fair gem away.

3. If thus the young hours have fleeted,
   When sorrow itself look'd bright,
   If thus the fair hope hath cheated,
   That led thee along so light,
   If thus the cold worlds now wither,
   Each feeling that once was dear,
   Come child of misfortune, come hither,
   I'll weep with thee, tear for tear.

Kate Kearney

Oh did you not hear of Kate Kear-ney? She lives on the banks

of Kil-lar-ney, From the glance of her eye, Shun dan-ger and

fly, For fat-als the glance of Kate Kear-ney.

Kate Kearney

1. Oh did you not hear of Kate Kearney?
   She lives on the banks of Killarney,
   From the glance of her eye,
   Shun danger and fly,
   For fatal's the glance of Kate Kearney.

2. For the eye is so modestly beaming,
   You ne'er think of mischief she's dreaming,
   Yet oh I can tell, how fatal the spell,
   That lurks in the eyes of Kate Kearney.

3. Oh should you e'er meet this Kate Kearney
   Who lives on the banks of Killarney
   Beware of her smile, for many a wile,
   Lies hid in the smile of Kate Kearney.

4. Tho' she looks so bewitchingly simply,
   Yet there's mischief in ev'ry dimple,
   And who dares inhale, her sighs spicy gale
   Must die by the breath of Kate Kearny.

Katey's Letter

Och girls dear did you ev-er hear I wrote my love a let-ter, And

al-though he cannot read, sure I thought twas all the bet-ter,

For why should he be puzzled with hard spelling in the mat-ter,

When the maning was so plain That I love him faith – ful-ly.   I

love him faith-ful-ly, and. he knows it, oh, he knows it, with-

out one word from me.

Katey's Letter

1. Och girls dear did you ever hear I wrote my love a letter,
   And although he cannot read, Sure I thought twas all the better,
   For why should he be puzzled with hard spelling in the matter,
   When the maning was so plain that I love him faithfully.
   I love him faithfully, and he knows it, oh, he knows it,
   Without one word from me.

2. I wrote it, and I folded it, and put a seal upon it,
   'Twas a seal almost as big, as the crown on my best bonnet,
   For I would not have the Post Master, make his remarks upon it
   As I said inside the letter that I loved him faithfully,
   I love him faithfully, and he knows it, oh he knows it,
   Without one word from me.

3. My heart was full, but when I wrote I dar'd not put the half in
   The neighbours know I love him, and they're mighty fond of chaffing
   So I dared not write his name outside, for fear they would be laughing,
   So I wrote „From little Kate to one whom she loves faithfully,
   I love him faithfully, and he knows it, oh he knows it,
   Without one word from me.

4. Now girls would you believe it, that postman so consated,
   No answer will he bring to me, so long as I have waited;
   But maybe there may not be one for the rason that I stated
   That my love can neither read nor write, but he loves me faithfully.
   He loves me faithfully, and I know where'er my love is
   That he is true to me.

Kitty of Coleraine

As beauti-ful Kit-ty one morning was tripping With a pitcher of

milk from the fair of Cole-raine, When she saw me she stumbled,

the pitch-er it tumbled, And all the sweet but-ter-milk water'd

the plain. Oh! what shall I do now, 'twas looking at you now,

Sure such a fine pitcher I'll ne'er see a-gain, 'Twas the pride

of my dai-ry, Oh! Bar-ney McClea-ry you-re sent as a plague to

the girls of Coleraine.

Kitty of Coleraine

1. As beautiful Kitty one morning was tripping
   With a pitcher of milk from the fair of Coleraine,
   When she saw me she stumbled, the pitcher it tumbled,
   And all the sweet buttermilk water'd the plain.
   Oh! what shall I do now, 'twas looking at you now,
   Sure such a fine pitcher I'll ne'er see again,
   'Twas the pride of my dairy,
   Oh! Barney McCleary you're sent as a plague
   To the girls of Coleraine.

2. I sat down beside her, and gently did chide her,
   That such a misfortune, should give her such pain,
   A kiss then I gave her, and before I did leave her,
   She vow'd for such pleasure, she'd break it again.
   'Twas haymaking season, I can't tell the reason,
   Misfortune, will never come single 'tis plain,
   For very soon after poor Kitty's disaster,
   The devil a pitcher was whole in Coleraine.

Love Is Pleasin'

O love is pleas-in' and love is teas-in' And love's a plea-sure

when first it is new; But as love grows old-er, at length grows

colder, And fades a-way like the morn-ing dew.

Love Is Pleasin'

1. O love is pleasin' and love is teasin'
   And love's a pleasure when first it is new;
   But as love grows older, at length grows colder
   And fades away like the morning dew.

2. I left my mother, I left my father,
   I left my brother and my sisters, too,
   I left my home and my kind relations,
   I left them all for the love of you.

3. If I'd a-knowed before I courted,
   That love had a-been such a killin' crime,
   I'd a-locked my heart in a box of gold,
   And tied it up with a silver twine.

4. O love is pleasin' and love is teasin'
   And love's a pleasure when first it is new,
   But as love grows older, at length grows colder,
   And fades away like the mornin' dew.

Love's Young Dream

Oh the days are gone when beau-ty bright, My heart's chaine

wove! When my dream of life from morn till night was love, still

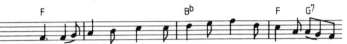

love! New hope may bloom, and days may come, Of mild-er calm-er

beam, But there's noth-ing half so sweet in life as Love's

Young Dream. But there's noth-ing half so sweet in life as

Love's Young Dream.

Love's Young Dream

1. Oh the days are gone when beauty bright, my heart's chaine wove!
   When my dream of life from morn till night was love, still love!
   New hope may bloom, and days may come,
   Of milder calmer beam,
   But there's nothing half so sweet in life as love's young dream.
   But there's nothing half so sweet in life as love's young dream.

2. Tho' the bard to purer fame may soar, when wild youth's past,
   Tho' he win the wise, who frowned before, to smile at last,
   He'll never meet a joy so sweet, in all his noon of fame,
   As when first he sang to woman's ear this soult-felt flame,
   And at ev'ry close, she blush'd to hear, the one lov'd name.

3. Now that hallow'd form is ne'er forgot, which first love traced,
   Still it lingering haunts the greenest spot, on mem'ry's waste,
   'Twas odour fled, as soon as shed, 'twas morning's winged dream,
   'Twas a light that ne'er can shine again, on life's dull stream.
   'Twas a light that ne'er can shine again, on life's dull stream.

Molly Brallaghan

Och man dear, did you ever hear of purty Molly Brallaghan, Ah,

wirras there she's left me, and I'll never be a man again, There's

not another summer's sun will e'er my poor hide tan again, Since

Molly she has left me all a-lone for to die. The place where my

poor heart was, you'd aisy roll a turnip in, 'Tis the size of

all Dublin and from Dublin to the "Devil's Glen" If she car'd

to take another sure she might have sent mine back again, And

not have left me by myself a-lone for to die.

Molly Brallaghan

1. Och man dear, did you ever hear of purty Molly Brallaghan,
   Ah, wirras there she's left me, and I'll never be a man again,
   There's not another summer's sun will e'er my poor hide tan again,
   Since Molly she has left me all alone for to die.
   The place where my poor heart was, you'd aisy roll a turnip in,
   'Tis the size of all Dublin and from Dublin to the „Devil's Glen"
   If she car'd to take another sure she might have sent mine back again,
   And not have left me by myself alone for to die.

2. Och man dear, I remember when the milking time was past and gone,
   We went into the meadows where she swore I was the only one,
   That ever she could love, yet oh! the base and cruel one,
   After that to leave me all alone for to die.
   Och man dear, I remember as we came home the rain began,
   And I rolled her in my freize coat, tho' ne'er a waistcoat I had on,
   My shirt was rather fine drawn and oh! the base and cruel one,
   After that to leave me all alone for to die.

3. I went and told my tale, to Father McDonnel, man,
   He bid me for to ax advice, of Counsellor McConnel, man;
   Who told me promise breaches, had been ever since the world began,
   Now I'd got only one pair, mam, and they're corduroy.
   Och mam now, what could he mean? Or what would you advise me to?
   Must my corduroys to Molly go? In troth I'm bothered what to do,
   I can't afford to lose my heart, and then to lose breeches too,
   Yet what need I be caring, when I've only to die.

4. The left side of my carcase is as weak as water gruel man,
   And nothing's left upon my bones, since Molly's been so cruel, man,
   I wish I had a blunder buss, I'd go and fight a duel man.
   Its better for to kill myself than stay here to die.
   I'm hot, and I'm determined, as any „Salamander" man.
   Won't you come to my wake, when I go my long meander man,
   I'll feel as valiant as the famour Alexander man.
   When I hear you crying round me, "Arrah why did you die?"

Mother Machree

I love the dear sil-ver that shines in your hair, And the brow

that's all fur-rowed, and wrink-led with care, I kiss the dear

fin-gers so toil-worn for me. Oh, God bless you and keep you,

Moth-er Ma-chree!

Mother Machree

I love the dear silver that shines in your hair,
And the brow that's all furrowed, and wrinkled with care,
I kiss the dear fingers so toilworn for me.
Oh, God bless you and keep you,
Mother Machree!

Norah, The Pride of Kildare

As beauteous as Flora is charming young Norah, The joy of my

heart, and the pride of Kildare: I ne'er will deceive her, for

sadly 'twould grieve her To find that I sighed for another less

fair; Her heart with truth teeming? Her eye with smiles beaming,

What mortal could injure a blossom so rare As Norah, dear Norah

the Pride of Kildare? Oh! Norah, dear Norah, the pride of Kildare.

Norah, The Pride of Kildare

1. As beauteous as Flora is charming young Norah,
   The joy of my heart, and the pride of Kildare:
   I ne'er will deceive her, for sadly 'twould grieve her
   To find that I sighed for another less fair;
   Her heart with truth teeming?
   Her eye with smiles beaming,
   What mortal could injure a blossom so rare
   As Norah, dear Norah the Pride of Kildare?
   Oh! Norah, dear Norah, the Pride of Kildare.

2. Where'er I may be love, I'll ne'er forget thee love,
   Tho' beauties may smile, and try to ensnare;
   Yet nothing shall ever, my heart from thee sever
   Dear Norah, sweet Norah, the pride of Kildare.
   Her heart with truth teeming, her eye with smiles beaming,
   What mortal could injure a blossom so rare
   As Norah, dear Norah, the Pride of Kildare,
   Oh! Norah, dear Norah, the Pride of Kildare.

Noreen Bawn

There's a glen in old Tir Connaill ⋮ There's a cot-tage in that

glen Where there dwelt an I-rish col-leen Who inspired the

hearts of men She was handsome hale and hearty Shy and

grace- ful like the dawn And they loved the wi-dow's daughter

Hand some laugh-ing Nor-een Bawn.

Noreen Bawn

1. There's a glen in old Tir Connaill
   There's a cottage in that glen
   Where there dwelt an Irish colleen
   Who inspired the hearts of men
   She was handsome hale and hearty
   Shy and graceful like the dawn
   And they loved the widow's daughter
   Handsome laughing Noreen Bawn.

2. Till one day there came a letter
   With her passage paid to go
   To the land where the Missouri
   And the Mississippi flow.
   So she said good-bys to Erin,
   And next morning with the dawn
   This poor widow broken hearted
   Parted with her Noreen Bawn.

3. Many years the widow waited;
   Till one morning to her door
   Came a tender hearted woman
   Costly were the clothes the wore,
   Saying „Mother, don't you know me,
   Tho' I'm frail tis but a cold".
   But her cheeks were flushed and scarlet
   And another tale they told.

4. There's a grave-yard in Tir Connaill
   Where the flowers wildly wave.
   There's a grey haired mother kneeling
   O'er a green and lonely grave.
   And "My 'Noreen" she is saying
   "It's been lonely since you've gone.
   T'was the curse of immigration
   Laid you here my Noreen Bawn."

5. Now fond youths and tender maidens
   Ponder well before you go
   From your humble homes in Erin,
   What's beyond you'll never know.
   What is gold and what is silver
   When your health and strength are gone,
   When they speak of immigration
   Won't you think of Noreen Bawn.

Rory O'More

Young Rory O'More courted Kathleen Bawn, He was bold as the hawk

She as soft as the dawn, He wish'd in his heart pretty Kathleen

to please, And he thought the best way to do that was to teaze;

"Now Rory be aisy", sweet Kathleen would cry, Reproof on her lip,

but a smile in her eye."With your tricks I don't know, in troth,

what I'm about. Faith you've teas'd till I've put on my cloak

inside out", "Oh jewel," says Rory, "that same is the way You've

thrated my heart for this many a day, And 'tis plaz'd that I am,

and why not, to be sure? For 'tis all for good luck", says bold

Ro-ry O'More.

Rory O'More

1. Young Rory O'More courted Kathleen Bawn,
   He was bold as the hawk
   She as soft as the dawn,
   He wish'd in his heart pretty Kathleen to please,
   And he thought the best way to do that was to teaze;
   "Now Rory be aisy", sweet Kathleen would cry,
   Reproof on her lip, but a smile in her eye.
   "With your tricks I don't know, in troth, inside out",
   "Oh jewel," says Rory, "that same is the way
   You've thrated my heart for this many a day,
   And 'tis plaz'd that I am, and why not, to be sure?
   For 'tis all for good luck", says bold Rory O'More.

2. "Indeed then", says Kathleen, "don't think of the like
   For I half gave a promise to soothering Mike;
   The ground that I walk on, he loves I'll be bound
   "Faith", says Rory, "I'd rather love you than the ground."
   "Now Rory I'll cry if you don't let me go
   Sure I dream every night that I'm hating you so."
   "Oh", says Rory, "that same I'm delighted to hear
   For dreams always go by contrairies my dear.
   Oh jewel, keep dreaming the same till you die
   And black morning will give dirty night the black lie
   And 'tis pleased that I am, and why not to be sure?
   Since it's all for good luck", says bold Rory O'More.

3. "Arrah, Kathleen, my darling, you've teased me enough
   Sure I've thrashed for your sake, Dinny Grimes, and Jim Duff,
   And I've made myself, drinking your health, quite a baste,
   So I think after that I may talk to the priest."
   Then Rory the rogue stole his arm round her neck,
   So soft, and so white, without freckle or speck,
   And he looked in her eyes, that were beaming with light,
   And he kissed her sweet lips, don't you think he was right?
   "Now Rory leave off sir, you'll hug me no more,
   That's eight times to-day that you've kissed me before",
   "Then here goes another", says he, "to make sure,
   For there's luck in odd numbers", says Rory O'More.

Saint Patrick Was A Gentleman

Saint Patrick was a gentleman He came of decent people, In Dub-

lin town he built a church, And up-on it put a steeple His fath-

er was a Callaghan, His mother was a Brady, His aunt was an O'

Shaughnessy, And his uncle was a Grady Then success to bold Saint

Patrick's fist, He was a Saint so clever He gave the snakes, And

toads a twist, And ban-ish'd them for ev-er.

Saint Patrick Was a Gentleman

1. Saint Patrick was a gentleman
   He came of decent people,
   In Dublin town he built a church,
   And upon it put a steeple
   His father was a Callaghan,

His mother was a Brady,
His aunt was an O'Shaughnessy,
And his uncle was a Grady,
Chorus
Then success to bold Saint Patrick's fist,
He was a Saint so clever
He gave the snakes,
And toads a twist,
And banish'd them for ever.

2. There's not a mile in Irelands Isle,
Where dirty vermin musters.
Where'er he put his dear forefoot,
Me murdered them in clusters.
The toads went hop, the frogs went plop,
Slapdash into the water;
And the beasts committed suicide,
To save them from the slaughter.
Chorus

3. Nine hundred thousand vipers blue,
He charmed with sweet discourses
And dined on them at Killaloo,
In soups, and second courses.
When blind worms, crawling on the grass
Disgusted all the nation,
He gave them a rise, and opened their eyes
To a sense of their situation.
Chorus

4. No wonder that our Irish boys,
Should be so free and frisky,
For Saint Patrick taught them first,
The joys of tippling with the whiskey.
No wonder that the Saint himself,
To taste it should be willing.
For his mother kept a shebeen shop,
In the town of Enniskillen.
Chorus

5. The Wicklow hills are very high,
   And so's the hill of Howth sir,
   But there's a hill much higher still,
   ay' higher than them both sir.
   'Twas on the top of this high hill,
   Saint Patrick preached the sarment,
   He drove the frogs into the bogs,
   And bothered all the varment.
Chorus

Savourneen Deelish

Oh the moment was sad when my love and I part-ed, Sa-vour-neen,

Dee-lish Ei-leen oge As I kiss'd off her tears I was nigh brok-

en heart-ed Sa-vour-neen Dee-lish Ei-leen oge. Wan was her cheek

which hung on my shoul-der Damp was her hand, no mar-ble was

cold-er, I felt that I never again should be-hold her Sa-vour-

neen Dee-lish Ei-leen oge.

Savourneen Deelish

1. Oh the moment was sad when my love and I parted,
   Savourneen, Deelish Eileen oge
   As I kiss'd off her tears I was nigh broken hearted
   Savourneen Deelish Eileen oge.
   Wan was her cheek which hung on my shoulder

   Damp was her hand, no marble was colder,
   I felt that I never again should behold her
   Savourneen Deelish Eileen oge.

2. When the word of command put our men into motion,
   Savourneen Deelish, Eileen oge,
   I buckled my knapsack to cross the wide ocean,
   Savourneen Deelish, Eileen oge.
   Brisk were our troops all roaring like thunder,
   Pleas'd with the voyage impatient for plunder
   My bosom with grief, was almost torn asunder,
   Savourneen Deelish, Eileen oge.

3. Long I fought for my country, tho' far my from true love,
   Savourneen Deelish, Eileen oge;
   All my pay and my booty I hoarded for you love,
   Savourneen Deelish, Eileen oge.
   Peace was proclaim'd, escap'd from the slaughter.
   Landed at home my sweet girl I sought her.
   But sorrow alas, to her cold grave, had brought her
   Savourneen Deelish, Eileen oge.

Teddy O'Neale

I've come to the cabin, he danc'd his wild jigs in, As neat a

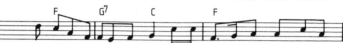

mudpalace as ever was seen and con-sid'ring it served to keep

poultry and pigs in, I'm sure it was alwaysmost el-e-gant clean!

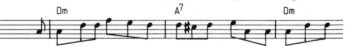

But now, all about it seems lonely and dreary, All sad and all

silent, no piper, no reel; Not even the sun, thro' the casement

is cheery, Since I miss the dear, darling boy, TeddyO'Neale.

Teddy O'Neale

1. I've come to the cabin, he danc'd his wild jigs in,
   As neat a mud palace as ever was seen and consid'ring
   It served to keep poultry and pigs in,
   I'm sure it was always most elegant clean!
   But now, all about it seems lonely and dreary,
   All sad and all silent, no piper, no reel;
   Not even the sun, thro' the casement is cheery,
   Since I miss the dear, darling boy, Teddy O'Neale.

2. I dreamt but last night, (Oh! bad luck to my dreaming,
   I'd die if I thought 'twould come surely to pass.)
   But I dreamt, while the tears, down my pillow were streaming,
   That Teddy was courtin' another fair lass.
   Och! did not I wake with a weeping and wailing,
   The grief of that thought, was too deep to conceal;
   My mother cried "Norah, child, what is your ailing?"
   And all I could utter, was "Teddy O'Neale".

3. Shall I ever forget, when the big ship was ready
   The moment had come, when my love must depart,
   How I sobb'd like a spalpeen, "Goodbye to you Teddy",
   With drops on my cheek and a stone at my heart.
   He says 'tis to better his fortune he's roving,
   But what would be gold, to the joy I would feel
   If I saw him come back to me, honest and loving
   Still poor, but my own darling Teddy O'Neale.

The Angels' Whisper

A ba-by was sleep-ing It's Mo-ther was weep-ing, For her husband

was far on the wild rag-ing sea; And the tem-pest was swell-ing

round the fish-er-man's dwelling, And she cried „Der-mot, dar-

ling;   Oh! come back to me."

The Angels' Whisper

1. A baby was sleeping
   It's Mother was weeping,
   For her husband was far on the wild raging sea;
   And the tempest was swelling round the fisherman's dwelling,
   And she cried „Dermot, darling; Oh! come back to me."

2. Her beads, while she numbered, the baby still slumbered
   And smiled in her face, as she bended her knee:
   Oh bless'd be that warning, my child thy sleep adorning,
   For I know that the Angels are whispering with thee.

3. And while they are keeping bright watch o'er thy sleeping,
   Oh pray to them softly my baby with me,
   And say thou would'st rather they'd watch o'er thy father,
   For I know that the Angels are whispering with thee.

4. The dawn of the morning, saw Dermot returning
   And the wife wept with joy her babe's father to see,
   And closely caressing her child with a blessing,
   She said "I knew that the Angels were whispering with thee."

The Boys From The County Armagh

There's one fair County in Ireland With mem'ries so

glorious and grand; Where nature has lavished its beauty

In the orchards of Erin's green land. I love its Cath-e-dral

city, One founded by Patrick so true; And it bears in the

hearts of its bosom The ashes of Bri-an Bo-ru. It's my own

I-rish home Far across the foam; Al-though I've oft times

left it In foreign lands to roam; No matter where I wander

Through cities near or far   My heart is at home in old

Ireland,   In the county of Ar-magh.

The Boys from the County Armagh

1. There's one fair County in Ireland
   With mem'ries so glorious and grand;
   Where nature has lavished its beauty
   In the orchards of Erin's green land.
   I love its Cathedral city,
   One founded by Patrick so true;
   And it bears in the hearts of its bosom
   The ashes of Brian Boru.
Chorus
   It's my own Irish home
   Far across the foam;
   Although I've oft times left it
   In foreign lands to roam;
   No matter where I wander
   Through cities near or far
   My heart is at home in old Ireland,
   In the county of Armagh.

2. I've travelled that part of the County,
   Through Newton, Forkhill, Crossmaglen;
   Around by the gap of Mount Norris
   And home by Blackwater again;
   Where girls are so gay and so hearty,
   None fairer you'll find near or far;
   But where are the boys that can court them
   Like the Boys from the County Armagh.
Chorus ...

The Irish Emigrant

I'm sit-ting on the stile Ma-ry, where we sat side by side, On a

bright May morn-ing, long a-go, when first you were my bride,

The corn was springing fresh and green and the lark sang loud

and high, And the red was on your lip Ma-ry, And the love light

in your eye. The place is lit-tle chang'd, Ma-ry, the day is

bright as then, The lark's loud song is in my ear, and the corn

is green a-gain. But I miss the soft clasp of your hand, and

your breath warm on my cheek, and I still keep list'ning to the

words, you nevermore may speak, You nevermore may speak.

The Irish Emigrant
(I'm sitting on the stile, Mary)

1. I'm sitting on the stile Mary, where we sat side by side,
   On a bright May morning, long ago, when first you were my bride,
   The corn was springing fresh and green and the lark sang loud and high,
   And the red was on your lip Mary,
   And the love light in your eye.
   The place is little chang'd, Mary,
   The day is bright as then,
   The lark's loud song is in my ear,
   And the corn is green again
   But I miss the soft clasp of your hand,
   And your breath warm on my cheek,
   And I still keep list'ning to the words,
   You never more may speak,
   You never more may speak.

2. I'm very lonely now Mary, for the poor make no new friends,
   But oh they love the better still, the few our Father sends,
   And you were all I had Mary, my blessing and my pride,
   There's nothing else to care for now, since my poor Mary died,
   I'm bidding you a long farewell, my Mary kind and true,
   But I'll not forget you darlin' in the land I'm going to,
   They say there's bread and work for all, and the sun shines always there,
   But I'll ne'er forget old Ireland, where it's fifty times as fair,
   Where it's fifty times as fair.

The Last Rose of Summer

'Tis the last rose of summer Left bloom-ing a-lone, All her love-

ly com-panions Are fad-ed and gone! No flow'r of her kind-red,

No rose bud is nigh, To re-flect back her blushes, Or give sigh

for sigh.

The Last Rose of Summer

1. 'Tis the last rose of Summer left blooming alone,
   All her lovely companions are faded and gone!
   No flow'r of her kindred, no rose bud is nigh,
   To reflect back her blushes, or give sigh for sigh.

2. I'll not leave thee there lone one, to pine on the stem
   Since the lovely are sleeping, go sleep thou with them:
   Thus kindly I scatter thy leaves o'er the bed,
   Where thy mates of the garden, lie scentles and dead.

3. So soon may I follow when friendships decay,
   And from love's shining circle the gems drop away,
   When true hearts lie wither'd, and fond ones are flown,
   Oh! who would inhabit this bleak world alone?

The Low Back'd Car

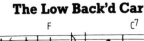

When first I saw sweet Peg-gy, 'Twas on a mar-ket day A low

back'd car she drove and sat Up-on a truss of hay: But when that

hay was bloom-ing grass, And deck'd with flow'rs of spring   No

flow'r was there, that could com-pare, To the blooming girl I

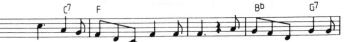

sing, As she sat in her low back'd car The man at the turnpike

bar,   Nev-er ask'd for the toll, But just rubb'd his old poll,

And look'd af-ter the low back'd car.

The Low Back'd Car

1. When first I saw sweet Peggy,
    'Twas on a market day
    A low back'd car she drove and sat
    Upon a truss of hay:
    But when that hay was blooming grass,
    And deck'd with flow'rs of spring
    No flow'r was there, that could compare,
    To the blooming girl I sing,
    As she sat in her low back'd car
    The man at the turnpike bar,
    Never ask'd for the toll,
    But just rubb'd his old poll,
    And look'd after the low back'd car.

2. In battle's wide commotion,
    The proud and mighty Mars,
    With hostile scythes demand his tythes
    Of death, in war-like cars.
    But Peggy, peaceful goddes,
    Has darts in her bright eye,
    That knock men down in the market town.
    As right and left they fly!
Chorus
    While she sits in her low back'd car,
    The battle more dangerous far,
    For the doctor's art, cannot cure the heart,
    That is hit from the low back'd car.

The Young May Moon

The young May moon is beaming love, The glow-worm's lamp is

gleaming love, How sweet to rove, thro' Mor-na's grove While the

drow-sy world is dreaming love, Then a-wake! the heav'ns look

bright my dear! 'Tis never too late for de-light, my dear! And

the best of all ways To lengthen our days, Is to steal a few

hours from the night my dear!

The Young May Moon

1. The young May moon is beaming love,
   The glowworm's lamp is gleaming love,
   How sweet to rove, thro' Mor-na's grove
   While the drowsy world is dreaming love,
   Then awake! The heav'ns look bright my dear!
   'Tis never too late for delight, my dear!
   And the best of all ways to lengthen our days,
   Is to steal a few hours from the night my dear!

2. Now all the world is sleeping, love.
   But the Sage, his star watch is keeping love,
   And I, whose star more glorious far,
   Is the eye, from that casement peeping love,
   Then awake! till rise of Sun my dear,
   The Sage's glass wi'll shun my dear,
   Or in watching the flight of bodies of light,
   He may happen to take thee from me, my dear.

When Irish Eyes Are Smiling

When I - rish eyes are smil - ing, Sure it's like a morn in Spring. In the lilt of I - rish laugh - ter you can hear the an - gels sing. When I - rish hearts are hap - py; All the world seems bright and gay, And when I - rish eyes are smil - ing, Sure they steal your heart a - way.

When Irish Eyes Are Smiling

When Irish eyes are smiling,
Sure it's like a morn in Spring.
In the lilt of Irish laughter
You can hear the angels sing.
When Irish hearts are happy;
All the world seems bright and gay,
And when Irish eyes are smiling,
Sure they steal your heart away.

Words spoken:
There are tears in your eyes, and I'm wondering why,
For it never should be there at all.
And with such sweet lilting laughter,
Like some fairy song,
And your eyes sparkling bright as can be;
With such power in your smile,
Sure a stone you would beguile,
And there never a tear drop should fall.
You should laugh all the while and other times smile,
And now smile a smile for me:

Chorus
When Irish eyes are smiling,
Sure it's like a morn in Spring.
In the lilt of Irish laughter
You can hear the angels sing.
When Irish hearts are happy;
All the world seems bright and gay,
And when Irish eyes are smiling,
Sure they steal your heart away.

Widow Machree

Widow Machree, it's no wonder you frown, Och hone! Widow Machree,

Faith it ru-ins your looks, that same ditty black gown. Och hone!

Widow Machree, How altered your air, With that close cap you

wear', Tis de-stroying your hair which should be flowing free;

Be no longer a churl, of its black silken curl, Och hone!

Widow Machree.

Widow Machree

1. Widow Machree, it's no wonder your frown,
   Och hone! Widow Machree,
   Faith it ruins your looks, that same ditty black gown.
   Och hone! Widow Machree,
   How altered your air,
   With that close cap you wear',

Tis destroying your hair
Which should be flowing free;
Be no longer a churl, of its black silken curl,
Och hone! Widow Machree.

2. Widow Machree, now the summer is come,
Och hone! Widow Machree,
When everything smiles, should beauty look glum?
Och hone! Widow Machree,
Sure the birds go in pairs, and the rabbits and hares,
Why even the bears now in couples agree;
And the mute little fish, tho' they can't speak they wish,
Och hone! Widow Machree.

3. Widow Machree, and when winter comes in,
Och hone! Widow Machree,
To be poking the fire all alone is a sin,
Och hone! Widow Machree,
Sure the shovel and tongs to each other belongs,
While the kettle sings songs full of family glee,
Yet alone with your cup, like a hermit you sup,
Och hone! Widow Machree.

4. And how do you know, with the comforts I've towld,
Och hone! Widow Machree!
But you're keeping some poor fellow out in the cowld,
Och hone! Widow Machree,
With such sins on your head, sure your peace would be fled
Could you sleep in your bed without thinking to see
Some ghost or some sprite that would wake you each night crying
Och hone! Widow Machree.

5. Then take my advice, darling Widow Machree,
Och hone, Widow Machree,
And with my advice, faith, I wish you'd take me,
Och hone! Widow Machree,
You'd have me to desire, then, to stir up the fire,
And sure hope is no liar in whisp'ring to me
That the ghosts would depart when you'd me near your heart,
Och hone! Widow Machree.

Love Songs

Barney O'Hea

Now let me a-lone, tho' I know you won't, I know you won't, I

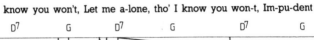

know you won't, Let me a-lone, tho' I know you won-t, Im-pu-dent

Bar-ney O'-Hea.   It makes me outrageous, when you're so conta-

gious, And you'd better look out for the stout Corney Creagh,

For he is the boy that be-lieves I'm his joy, So you'd bet-ter

be-have yourself, Barney O'Hea, Im-pu-dent Bar-ney,

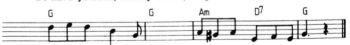

None of your Blar-ney,   Im-pu-dent Bar-ney O'Hea.

Barney O'Hea

1. Now let me alone, tho' I know you won't,
   I know you won't, I know you won't,
   Let me alone, tho' I know you won't,
   Impudent Barney O'Hea.
   It makes me outrageous, when you're so contagious,
   And you'd better look out for the stout Corney Creagh,
   For he is the boy that believes I'm his joy,
   So you'd better behave yourself, Barney O'Hea,
   Impudent Barney, None of your Blarney,
   Impudent Barney O'Hea.

2. I hope you're not going to Bandon fair,
   To Bandon fair, to Bandon fair,
   Indeed I'm not wanting to meet you there
   Impudent Barney O'Hea.
   For Corney's at Cork, and my brother's at work,
   And my mother sits spinning at home all day.
   So no one will be there, of poor me to take care,
   So I hope you won't follow me Barney O'Hea.
   Impudent Barney O'Hea, None of your Blarney;
   Impudent Barney O'Hea.

3. But as I was walking up Bandon Street,
   Up Bandon Street, up Bandon Street,
   Just who do you think, that myself should meet
   But impudent Barney O'Hea.
   He said I look'd killin' I call'd him a villain,
   And bid him that minute get out of my way,
   He said I was joking, and grinned so provoking,
   I could not help laughing with Barney O'Hea.
   Impudent Barney O'Hea, None of your Blarney,
   Impudent Barney O'Hea.

4. He knew 'twas all right, when he saw me smile,
   He saw me smile, he saw me smile,
   For he is a rogue to every wile,
   Impudent Barney O'Hea.
   He coaxed me to choose him, For if I'd refuse him,
   He swore he'd kill Corney the very next day
   So far fear 'twould go further, and just to stay murder

   I think I must marry that mad-cap O'Hea,
   Bothering Barney, he has the Blarney
   To make a girl Mistress O'Hea.

Believe Me If All Those Endearing Young Charms

Be - lieve me, if all those en-dearing young charms which I

gaze on so foundly to-day   Were to change by to-mor-row and

fleet in my arms, like fair-y gifts   fad-ing a-way. Thou would

still   be a-dored as this mo-ment thou art, let thy lov-li-ness

fade as it will   And a-round the dear ruin each wish of my

heart would en-twine it-self   ver-dant-ly still.

Believe Me If All Those Endearing Young Charms

1. Believe me, if all those endearing young charms
   Which I gaze on so foundly today
   Were to change by tomorrow and fleet in my arms,
   Like fairy gifts fading away.
   Thou would still be adored as this moment thou art,
   Let thy lovliness fade as it will
   And a round the dear ruin each wish of my heart
   Would entwine itself verdantly still.

2. It is not while beauty and youth are thine own,
   And thy cheeks unprofaned by a tear,
   That the fervour and faith of a soul can be known
   To which time will but make thee more dear.
   Oh! the heart that has truly loved never forgets,
   But as truly loves on to the close, –
   As the sunflower turns on her God when he sets,
   The same look that she gave when he rose.

Develish Mary

lustig

I went up to Lon-don town to court a fair young la-dy, I in-quired a-bout her name, and they called her Dev-il-ish Ma-ry.

Come-a fa-la -ling, come-a-ling, come-a-ling, Come-a -fa-la-ling, come-a-der-ry.

Aus: „Our singing country", von John und Alan Lomax (Macmillian N.Y., 1941). Gesungen von Jesse Stafford, Crowley, La., 1934. Peter Kennedy hat in Irland auch ähnliche Stücke gefunden z.B. „The wearing of the Breeches".

Develish Mary

1. I went up to London town
   To court a fair young lady,
   I inquired about her name,
   And they called her Devilish Mary.
Chorus
   Come-a-fa-la-ling, come-a-ling, come-a-ling,
   Come-a-fa-la-ling, come-a-der-ry.

2. We sat down to courtin'
   She got up in a hurry.
   Made it all up into her mind
   To marry the very next Thursday.
Chorus ...

3. Well, she filled my heart with sadness,
   She sewed my side with stitches,
   She jumped and kicked and popped her heels
   And swore she'd wear my britches.
Chorus ...

4. One day I said to Mary,
   We'd better be parted,
   No sooner had I said the word,
   Than she bundled up her clothes and started.
Chorus ...

5. If ever I marry in this wide world,
   It'll be for love, not riches,
   Marry a little girl about four feet high
   So she can't wear my britches.
Chorus ...

I'll Take You Home Again, Kathleen

I' ll take you home a-gain, Kath-leen, A-cross the o-cean wild and

wide, To where your heart has ev-er been, Since first you were

my bon-ny bride. The ro-ses all have left your cheek, I've watch'd

them fade a-way and die: Your voice is sad whene'er you speak

And tears be-dim your lov-ing eyes. Oh! I will take you back,

Kath-leen, To where your heart will find no pain, And when the

fields are fresh and green I'll take you to your home a-gain.

I'll Take You Home Again, Kathleen

1. I'll take you home again, Kathleen,
   Across the ocean wild and wide,
   To where your heart has ever been,
   Since first you were my bonny bride.
   The roses all have left your cheek,
   I've watch'd them fade away and die:
   Your voice is sad whene'er you speak
   And tears bedim your loving eyes.
   Oh! I will take you back, Kathleen,
   To where your heart will find no pain,
   And when the fields are fresh and green
   I'll take you to your home again.

2. I know you love me, Kathleen, dear,
   Your heart was ever fond and true;
   I always feel when you are near,
   That life holds nothing dear but you.
   The smiles that once you gave to me,
   I scarcely ever see them now;
   Though many, many times I see
   A dark'ning shadow on your brow.
   Chorus ...

3. To that dear home beyond the sea,
   My Kathleen shall again return,
   And when thy old friends welcome thee,
   Thy loving heart will cease to yearn.
   Where laughs the little silver stream,
   Beside your mother's humble cot,
   And brightest rays of sunshine gleam,
   There all your grief will be forgot.
   Chorus ...

Kate O'Shane

The cold winds of Au-tumn, wail mournful -ly here, The leaves

round me fal -ling, are fad-ed and sere, But chill tho' the

breeze be, and threat'ning the storm, My heart full of fondness,

beats kind-ly and warm, Oh Dennis dear come back to me, I count

the hours away from thee; Re-turn, oh never part a-gain, From

thy own dar-ling Kate O'Shane.

Kate O'Shane

1. The cold winds of Autumn, wail mournfully here,
   The leaves round me falling, are faded and sere,
   But chill tho' the breeze be, and threat'ning the storm,
   My heart full of fondness, beats kindly and warm.
   Oh Dennis dear come back to me,
   I count the hours away from thee;
   Return, oh never part again,
   From thy own darling Kate O'Shane.

2. 'Twas here we last parted, 'twas there we first met,
   And ne'er has he caused me one sigh of regret;
   Though seasons may alter, their change I defy,
   My heart's one glad summer when Dennis is by.
   Oh Dennis dear, come back to me,
   I count the hours away from thee,
   Return, oh never part again
   From thy own darling Kate O'Shane.

Kathleen Mavourneen

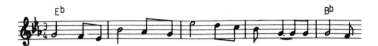

Kath-leen Ma-vour-neen! The grey dawn is break-ing, The horn of

the hun-ter is heard on the hill: The lark from her light wing

the bright dew is shak-ing Kath-leen Ma-vour-neen! what, slum-

b'ring still? Oh! hast thou for-got-ten how soon we must sev-er?

Oh! hast thou for-got-ten this day we must part, It may be for

years and it may be for ev-er, Oh! why art thou si-lent, thou

voice of my heart, It may be for years and it may be for ev-er,

The why art thou si-lent Kath-leen Ma-vour-neen.

Kathleen Mavourneen

1. Kathleen Mavourneen! The grey dawn is breaking,
   The horn of the hunter is heard on the hill:
   The lark from her light wing the bright dew is shaking
   Kathleen Mavourneen! what, slumb'ring still?
   Oh! hast thou forgotten how soon we must sever?
   Oh! hast thou forgotten this day we must part,
   It may be for years and it may be for ever,
   Oh! why art thou silent, thou voice of my heart,
   It may be for years and it may be for ever,
   The why art thou silent Kathleen Mavourneen.

2. Kathleen Mavourneen, awake from thy slumbers
   The blue mountains glow in the sun's golden light
   Ah! where is the spell that once hung on thy numbers?
   Arise in thy beauty, thou star of my night.
   Mavourneen, Mavourneeen, my sad tears are falling,
   To think that from Erin und thee I must part;
   It may be for years, and it may be for ever;
   Then why art thou silent, thou voice of my heart?
   It may be for years, and it may be for ever;
   Then why art thou silent, Kathleen Mavourneen?

Molly Bawn

Oh Molly Bawn, why leave me pin-ing, All lonely waiting here for

you? While the stars a-bove are bright-ly shin-ing Be-cause

they've nothing else to do. The flowers late were o-pen

keep-ing, To try a ri-val blush with you, But their mo-ther,

Na-ture, set them sleep-ing, With their ro-sy fa-ces wash'd with

dew. Oh! Molly Bawn, why leave me pin-ing, All lonely waiting

here for you? The stars a-bove are sweetly shining, Be-cause

they've nothing else to do, Mol-ly Bawn, Mol-ly Bawn.

Molly Bawn

1. Oh Molly Bawn, why leave me pining,
   All lonely waiting here for you?
   While the stars above are brightly shining
   Because they've nothing else to do.
   The flowers late were open keeping,
   To try a rival blush with you,
   But their mother, Nature, set them sleeping,
   With their rosy faces wash'd with dew.
   Oh! Molly Bawn, why leave me pining,
   All lonely waiting here for you?
   The stars above are sweetly shining,
   Because they've nothing else to do,
   Molly Bawn, Molly Bawn.

2. Now the pretty flowers were made to bloom dear,
   And the pretty stars were made to shine,
   And the pretty girls were made for boys dear,
   And maybe you were made for mine.
   The wicked watchdog here is snarling,
   He takes me for a thief you see,
   For he knows I'll steal you, Molly darling,
   And then transported I should be.
   Oh! Molly Bawn, why leave me pining,
   All lonely waiting here for you?
   The stars above are sweetly shining,
   Because they've nothing else to do.
   Molly Bawn, Molly Bawn.

Robin Adair

What's this dull town to me? Ro-bin's not near; What was't I

wish'd to see? what wish'd to hear? Where all the joy and mirth,

Made this town heav'n on earth, O! they've all fled wi'thee,

Ro-bin A-dair.

Robin Adair

1. What's this dull town to me?
   Robin's not near;
   What was't I wish'd to see?
   What wish'd to hear?
   Where all the joy and mirth,
   Made this town heav'n on earth,
   O! they've all fled wi thee,
   Robin Adair.

2. What made th'assembly shine?
   Robin Adair.
   What made the ball so fine?
   Robin was there.
   And when the play was o'er
   What made my heart so sore?
   Oh! it was parting with
   Robin Adair.

3. But now thou'rt cold to me
   Robin Adair.
   And I no more shall see
   Robin Adair.
   Yet he I lov'd so well,
   Still in my heart shall dwell,
   Oh! I can ne'er forget
   Robin Adair.

Sweet Rosie O'Grady

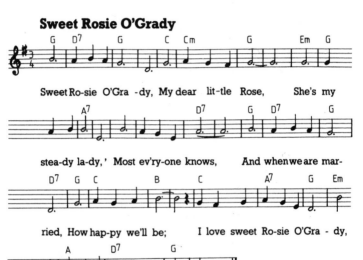

Sweet Ro-sie O'Gra -dy, My dear lit-tle Rose, She's my

stea-dy la-dy,' Most ev'ry-one knows, And when we are mar-

ried, How hap-py we'll be; I love sweet Ro-sie O'Gra - dy,

And Ro-sie O'Gra-dy loves me.

Sweet Rosie O'Grady

Sweet Rosie O'Grady,
My dear little Rose,
She's my steady lady,
Most ev'ryone knows,
And when we are married,
How happy we'll be;
I love sweet Rosie O'Grady,
And Rosie O'Grady loves me.

Terence's Farewell to Kathleen

So my Kathleen you're go-ing to leave my, All a-lone by my-self

in this place, But I'm sure that you'll ne-ver de-ceive me, Oh

no, if there's truth in that face, Tho' En-gland's a beautiful

country Full of Il -li-gant boys, Och! what then? You would not

for -get your poor Terence you'll back to old Ireland a-gain.

Terence's Farewell To Kathleen

1. So my Kathleen you're going to leave my,
   All alone by myself in this place,
   But I'm sure that you'll never deceive me,
   Oh no, if there's truth in that face,
   Tho' England's a beautiful country
   Full of Illigant boys, Och! what then?
   You would not forget your poor Terence
   You'll back to old Ireland again.

2. Och! them English, deceivers by nature,
   Tho' may be you'll think them sincere,

   They'll say you're a charming sweet creature,
   But don't you believe them my dear.
   No Kathleen, agrah, don't be minding,
   The flattering speeches they'll make,
   Just tell them a poor boy in Ireland,
   Is braking his heart for your sake.

3. Its a folly to keep you from going,
   Tho' faith, its a mighty hard case,
   For Kathleen you know, ther's no knowin',
   When next I may see your sweet face.
   And when you come back to me Kathleen,
   None the better shall I be off then,
   You'll be speaking such beautiful English,
   Sure, I won't know my Kathleen again.

4. Ah now what's the need of this hurry?
   Don't fluster me so in this way,
   I've forgot twixt the grief, and the flurry,
   Every word, I was meaning to say.
   Now, just wait a minute I bid ye,
   Can I talk if ye bother me so?
   Och, Kathleen my blessing go wi' ye,
   Every inch of the way that ye go.

The Girl I Left Behind Me

I'm lonesome since I cross'd the hill, and o'er the moor and

val-ley, Such heavy thoughts my heart do fill, Since parting

with my Sal-ly. I seek no more the fine and gay, for each but

does re-mind me, How swift the hours did pass a-way, With the

girl I left be-hind me.

The Girl I Left Behind Me

1. I'm lonesome since I cross'd the hill,
   And o'er the moor and valley,
   Such heavy thoughts my heart do fill,
   Since parting with my Sally.
   I seek no more the fine and gay,
   For each but does remind me,
   How swift the hours did pass away,
   With the girl I left behind me.

2. Oh, ne'er shall I forget the night,
   The stars were bright above me,

   And gently lent their silv'ry light,
   When first she vow'd she lov'd me,
   But now I'm bound for Brighton camp,
   Kind Heav'n may favour find me,
   And send me safely back again,
   To the girl I left behind me.

3. The bee shall honey taste no more,
   The dove become a ranger,
   The dashing waves shall cease to roar,
   E'er she's to me a stranger,
   The vows we've registered above me,
   Shall ever cheer and bind me,
   In constancy to her I love,
   The girl I left behind me.

The Rose of Tralee

The pale moon was rising a-bove the green mountain, The sun was

de-clining be-neath the blue sea, When I stray'd with my love

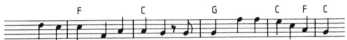

to the pure crystal fountain That stands in the beautiful vale

of Tra-lee. She was lovely and fair as the rose of the summer,

Yet 'twas not her beauty a-lone that won me, Oh, no 'twas the

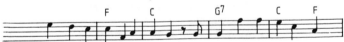

truth in her eye ever dawning, That made me love Ma-ry, the

Rose of Tra-lee.

The Rose of Tralee

1. The pale moon was rising above the green mountain,
   The sun was declining beneath the blue sea,
   When I stray'd with my love to the pure crystal fountain
   That stands in the beautiful vale of Tralee.
   She was lovely and fair as the rose of the summer,
   Yet 'twas not her beauty alone that won me,
   Oh, no 'twas the truth in her eye ever dawning,
   That made me love Mary, the Rose of Tralee.

2. The cool shades of ev'ning, their mantles were spreading,
   And Mary all smiling, sat list'ning to me,
   The moon thro' the valley, her pale rays were shedding
   When I won the heart of the Rose of Tralee.
   Tho' lovely and fair, as the Rose of the summer,
   Yet 'twas not her beauty alone that won me,
   Oh, no! 'twas the trust in her eye ever dawning,
   That made me love Mary the Rose of Tralee.

The Snowy-Breasted Pearl

There's a Colleen fair as May, for a year and for a day I have

sought by ev'ry way her heart to gain. There's no art of tongue

or eye fond youths with maidens try, But I've tried with cease-

less sigh yet tried in vain. If to France or off Spain she'd

cross the wat'ry main, To see her face again the seas I'd brave

And if 'tis heav'ns decree that mine she may not be May the Son

of Mar-y me in mer-cy save.

The Snowy-Breasted Pearl
(There's a Colleen fair as May)

1. There's a Colleen fair as May,
   For a year and for a day I have sought
   By ev'ry way her heart to gain.
   There's no art of tongue or eye fond youths with maidens try,
   But I've tried with ceaseless sigh yet tried in vain.
   If to France or off Spain she'd cross the wat'ry main,
   To see her face again the seas I'd brave
   And if 'tis heav'ns decree that mine she may not be
   May the Son of Mary me in mercy save.

2. Oh thou blooming milk-white dove to whom I've given true love,
   Do not ever thus reprove my constancy.
   There are maidens would be mine with wealth in land or kine,
   If my heart would but incline to turn from thee
   But a kiss with welcome bland and a touch of thy fair hand
   Are all that I demand would'st thou not spurn,
   For if not mine dear girl, oh snowy breasted pearl
   May I never from the fair with life return.

Treat My Daughter Kindly

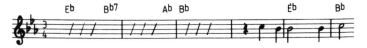

Well I once there was

a farmer a good old soul was he.   I used to work upon his farm

down in the count-ry   He had one only daughter and her chanced

to win   And when I asked him for her hand these words he did

begin.   "Oh treat my daughter kindly and shade her from all

harm.   Be-fore I die I'll will to you my little house and farm

My horse, my dog, my cow,   my bonny sheep and barn.

And all the little chickens in the gar - den."

Treat my daughter kindly

1. Well I once there was a farmer. A good old soul was he.
   I used to work upon his farm down in the country
   He had one only daughter and her chanced to win
   And when I asked him for her hand these words he did begin.
Chorus
   "Oh treat my daughter kindly and shade her from all harm.
   Before I die I'll will to you my little house and farm
   My horse, my dog, my cow, my bonny sheep and barn.
   And all the little chickens in the garden.

2. Well I loved this pretty girl and she loved me just the same.
   And when my daily work was done with her I would remain.
   To watch her milk her father's cow and shade her from all harm.
   And many's the glass of milk I had before I left the farm.
Chorus ...

3. Oh now that we are married and settled down for life.
   I often think of her old man and of his good advice
   To treat his daughter kindly and shade her from all harm.
   And now I am the owner of that little house and farm.
Chorus ...

Patriotic Songs

A Nation Once Again

When boy-hood's fire was in my blood, I read of an-cient free-

men; For Greece and Rome who brave-ly stood, Three hun-dred

men and three men, And there I prayed I yet might see, Our

fet- ters rent in twain, And Ire-land, long a pro-vince, Be a

Na-tion once a-gain. A Na-tion once a-gain, a Na-tion once a-

gain And Ire-land long a pro-vince, Be a Na-tion once a-gain

A Nation Once Again

1. When boyhood's fire was in my blood,
   I read of ancient freemen;
   For Greece and Rome who bravely stood,
   Three hundred men and three men,
   And there I prayed I yet might see,

Our fetters rent in twain,
And Ireland, long a province,
Be a Nation once again.
Chorus
    A Nation once again, a Nation once again
    And Ireland long a province,
    Be a Nation once again.

2. And from that time through wildest woe
    That hope has shone, a far light,
    Nor could Love's brightest summer glow,
    Outshine that solemn star light.
    It seemed to watch above my head,
    In forum field and fain,
    It's angel voice around my bed,
    A Nation once again.
Chorus
    A Nation once again, a Nation once again,
    It's angel voice around my bed,
    A Nation once again.

3. It whispered, too, that freedom's ark,
    And Service high and holy,
    Would be profaned by feelings dark,
    And fashion vain or lowly.
    For freedom comes from God's right hand,
    And needs a godly train
    And righteous men must make our land
    A Nation once again.
Chorus
    A Nation once again, a Nation once again,
    And righteous men must make our land,
    A Nation once again.

4. So as I grew from boy to man,
    I bent me to that bidding,
    My spirit of each selfish plan,
    And cruel fashion ridding,
    For thus I hope some day to aid,
    Oh! can such hope be vain,
    When my dear country should be made
    A Nation once again.

Chorus
    A Nation once again, a Nation once again,
    When my dear country should be made
    A Nation once again.

Let Erin* Remember The Days of Old

Let E-rin re-mem-ber the days of old, Ere her faith-less sons

be-tray'd her; When Ma-la-chi wore the col-lar of gold, Which he

won from the proud in-vad-er; When her Kings, with stan-dards of

green un-furl'd, Led the Red Branch knights to dan-ger; Ere the

em-'rald gem of the west-ern world, Was set in the crown of a

stranger.

Let Erin Remember The Days Of Old

1. Let Erin remember the days of old,
   Ere her faith-less sons betray'd her;
   When Malachi wore the collar of gold,
   Which he won from the proud invader;
   When her Kings, with standards of green unfurl'd,

   Led the Red Branch knights to danger;
   Ere the em'rald gem of the western world,
   Was set in the crown of a stranger.

2. On Lough Neagh's bank, as the fisherman strays,
   When the clear cold eve's declining,
   He sees the round towers of other days,
   In the wave beneath him shining.
   Thus shall mem'ry often in dreams sublime,
   Catch a glimpse of the days that are over;
   Thus sighing look thro' the Waves of Time,
   For the long faded glories they cover.

National Anthem

Sin-ne Fian-na Fail, a-ta faoi gheall ag Ei-rinn, Buion dar slua

thar toinn do rai - nig chughainn, Faoi mhoid bheith saor, Sean-

tir ar sin-sear feas-ta, Ni fhag-far faoin tior-an na faoin

traill.   A-nocht a theam sa bhear-na baoil, Le gean ar Ghaeil

chun bais no saoil, Le gun-na screach, faoi lamhach na bpi-lear,

Seo libh canaig amh-ran na   bhFiann.

National Anthem

Sinne Fianna Fail, ata faoi gheall ag Eirinn,
Buion dar slua thar toinn do rainig chughainn,
Faoi mhoid bheith saor, Seantir ar sinsear feasta,
Ni fhagfar faoin tioran na faoin traill.
Anocht a theam sa bhear-na baoil,
Le gean ar Ghaeil chun bais no saoil,
Le gunna screach, faoi lamhach na bpilear,
Seo libh canaig amhran na bhFiann.

Oft In The Stilly Night

Oft in the stil-ly night, Ere slum-ber's chain has bound me,

Fond mem-'ry brings the light of oth-er days a-round me. The

smiles, the tears of boy-hood's years, The words of love then

spoken; The eyes that shone now dimm'd and gone, The cheer-ful

hearts now bro-ken. Oft in the stilly night, Ere slumber's chain

has bound me, Fond mem-'ry brings the light of other days a-

round me.

Oft In The Stilly Night

1. Oft in the stilly night,
   Ere slumber's chain has bound me,
   Fond mem'ry brings the light
   Of other days around me.
   The smiles, the tears of boy-hood's years,
   The words of love then spoken;
   The eyes that shone now dimm'd and gone,
   The cheerful hearts now broken.
   Oft in the stilly night,
   Ere slumber's chain has bound me,
   Fond mem'ry brings the light
   Of other days around me.

2. When I remember all
   The friends so link'd together,
   I've seen around me fall,
   Like leaves in wintry weather,
   I feel like one who treads alone
   Some banquet hall deserted;
   Whose lights are fled, whose garlands dead,
   And all but he departed.
   Thus in the stilly night,
   Ere slumber's chains has bound me,
   Fond memory brings the light
   Of other days around me.

Slievenamon

All a-lone, all alone, by the seawash'd shore, All a-lone in the

fes- tive hall The great hall is gay, while the huge waves roar,

But my heart is not there at all. It flies far away, by the night

and the day; To the time and the joy that are gone, I never shall

forget the sweet maiden I met In the valley of Slievena-mon.

I never shall forget the sweet maiden I met In the valley of

Slievena-mon.

Slievenamon

1. All alone, all alone, by the seawash'd shore,
   All alone in the festive hall
   The great hall is gay, while the huge waves roar,
   But my heart is not there at all.
   It flies far away, by the night and the day;
   To the time and the joy that are gone,
   I never shall forget the sweet maiden I met
   In the valley of Slievenamon.
   I never shall forget the sweet maiden I met
   In the valley of Slievenamon.

2. In the festive hall by the seawashed shore,
   My restless spirit cries,
   "My love, oh my love shall I never see thee more
   My land, will you ever uprise?"
   By night and by day, I will ever, ever pray,
   As lonely this life goes on
   To see my flag unrolled, and my true love to enfold,
   In the valley of Slievenamon.

3. It was not the grace of a queenly air,
   Nor her cheeks of the roses' glow,
   Nor her soft dark eyes, nor her curling hair,
   Nor was it her lily white brow.
   'Twas the soul of truth, and melting ruth,
   Her smile like the summer's dawn
   That stole my heart away on that bright summer day,
   In the valley of Slievenamon.

The Harp That Once

The harp that once thro' Tar-a's halls, The soul of mu-sic shed,

Now hangs as mute on Tar-a's walls As if that soul were fled: So

sleeps the pride of for-mer days? So glo-ry's thrill is o'er,

And hearts that once beat high for praise Now feel that pulse

no more.

The Harp That Once

1. The harp that once thro' Tara's halls,
   The soul of music shed,
   Now hangs as mute on Tara's walls
   As if that soul were fled:
   So sleeps the pride of former days?
   So glory's thrill is o'er,
   And hearts that once beat high for praise
   Now feel that pulse no more.

2. No more to chiefs and ladies bright,
   The harp of Tara swells;
   The chord alone that breaks at night,
   Its tale of ruin tells:
   Thus freedom now so seldom wakes;
   The only throb she gives,
   Is when some heart indignant breaks,
   To show that still she lives.

The Minstrel Boy

The Min-strel boy to the war is gone, In the rank of death you'll

find him; His father's sword he has gird-ed on, And his wild

harp slung be-hind him. "Land of song!" said the war-rior bard,

"Tho'the world be-trays thee, One sword, at least, thy rights

shall guard, One faith- ful heart shall praise thee."

The Minstrel Boy

1. The Minstrel boy to the war is gone,
   In the rank of death you'll find him;
   His father's sword he has girded on,
   And his wild harp slung behind him.
   "Land of song!" said the warrior bard,
   "Tho'the world betrays thee,
   One sword, at least, thy rights shall guard,
   One faithful heart shall praise thee."

2. The minstrel fell; but the foeman's chain
   Could not bring that proud soul under;
   The harp he loved ne'er spoke again,
   For he tore its chords asunder;
   And said, "No chain shall sully thee
   Thou soul of love and bravery!
   Thy songs were made for the pure and free,
   They shall never sound in slavery."

The Wearin' O' The Green

Oh! Paddy dear, an' did you hear the news that's go-in' round?

The Shamrock is forbid by law to grow on I-rish ground! St. Pat-

rick's day no more we'll keep, his colour can't be seen, For

There's a cru-el law again the wearin' o' the green! I met wi'

Napper Tandy an' he took me by the hand An' he said, "How's poor

ould Ireland, an' how does she stand? She's the most distressful

country that ever yet was seen, For they're hangin' men and

124

women there for wearin' o' the green. She's the most distressful

country that ever yet was seen, For they're hangin' men and

women there for wearin' o' the green.

The Wearin' o' The Green

1. Oh! Paddy dear, an' did you hear the news that's go-in' round?
   The Shamrock is forbid by law to grow on Irish ground!
   St. Patrick's day no more we'll keep, his colour can't be seen,
   For there's a cruel law again the wearin' o' the green!
   I met wi' Napper Tandy an' he took me by the hand
   An' he said, "How's poor ould Ireland, an' how does she stand?
Chorus
   She's the most distressful country that ever yet was seen,
   For they're hangin' men and women there for wearin' o' the green.
   She's the most distressful country that ever yet was seen,
   For they're hangin' men and women there for wearin' o' the green.

2. Then since the colour we must wear, is England's cruel red,
   Sure Ireland's sons, will ne'er forget the blood that they have shed,
   You may pull she shamrock from your hat, and cast it on the sod,
   But 'twill take root, and flourish there, tho' underfoot 'tis trod,
   When laws can stop the blades of grass from growin' as they grow,
   And when the leaves in summer time, their verdure dare not show,
   Then I will change the colour too, and wear in my caubeen,
   But till that day please God, I'll stick to wearin' o' the green.
Chorus

3. But if at last the colour should be torn from Ireland's heart,
   Her sons with shame and sorrow, from the dear ould isle will part,
   I've heard the whisper of a land, that lies beyond the sea,
   Where rich and poor stand equal, in the light of freedom's day,
   Ah Erin must we leave you, driven by a tyrant's hand,
   Must we seek a mother's blessing from a strange and distant land,
   Where the cruel cross of England shall never more be seen,
   And where please God, we'll live and die, still wearin' o' the green.
Chorus

Songs of Home

A Little Bit of Heaven

Sure, a little bit of Heaven fell from out the sky one day, And

nestled on the o-cean in a spot so far away; And when the angels

found it, Sure it looked so sweet and fair, They said, "Suppose

we leave it, for it looks so peaceful there !" So they sprinkled

it with stardust just to make the shamrocks grow; 'Tis the only

place you'll find them, no matter where you go; Then they dot-

ted it with silver To make its lakes so grand, And when they

had it finished sure they called it Ireland.

A Little Bit Of Heaven

Sure, a little bit of Heaven fell from out the sky one day,
And nestled on the ocean in a spot so far away;
And when the angels found it,
Sure it looked so sweet and fair,
They said, "Suppose we leave it,
For it looks so peaceful there!"
So they sprinkled it with stardust
Just to make the shamrocks grow;
'Tis the only place you'll find them,
No matter where you go;
Then they dotted it with silver
To make its lakes so grand,
And when they had it finished
Sure they called it Ireland.

Barney Take Me Home Again

Oh Bar-ney dear, I'd give the world, to see my home a-cross the

sea, Where all the days were joy im-pearl'd Before I went to

roam with three I long be-neath its roof to rest, Where nev-er

comes a care or pain In all the earth it is the best, Oh

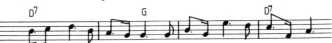

Bar-ney take me home a-gain. Oh take me home yes take me home,

to where my heart will know no pain, I'll go with three a-cross

the sea, Oh Bar-ney take me home a-gain.

132

Barney Take Me Home Again

1. Oh Barney dear, I'd give the world, to see my home across the sea,
   Where all the days were joy impearl'd
   Before I went to roam with three
   I long beneath its roof to rest,
   Where never comes a care or pain
   In all the earth it is the best,
   Oh Barney take me home again.
Chorus
   Oh take me home yes take me home,
   To where my heart will know no pain,
   I'll go with three across the sea,
   Oh Barney take me home again.

2. Oh Barney dear, in happy dreams,
   I live once more the dear old days,
   By flow'ry dells and sun kissed streams,
   Sweet recollection fondly strays;
   I see each well remember'd face
   And hear their voices' glad refrain
   As memory its step retrace,
   Oh Barney take me home again.
Chorus

3. Oh Barney dear, why did we roam
   To seek a fortune in the west?
   When love and peace in that old home,
   Were better far than all the rest
   For what is fame and wealth, and all,
   When life is dark with care or pain,
   The past is far beyond recall,
   Oh Barney take me home again.
Chorus

Come Back to Erin*

Come back to E-rin, Ma-vour-neen, Ma-vour-neen, Come back A-roon,

to the land of thy birth, Come with the sham-rocks and spring-

time, Ma-vour-neen, And it's Kil-lar-ney shall ring with our

mirth. Sure when we lent ye to beau-ti-ful Eng-land,

Lit- tle we thought of the lone win-ter days, Lit-tle we thought

of the hush of the star-shine O-ver the moun-tain, the Bluffs

and the Brays. Then come back to E-rin, Ma-vour-neen, Ma-vour-

neen, Come back a-gain to the land of thy brith; Come back to

E-rin, Ma-vour-neen, Ma-vour-neen And it's Kil-lar-ney shall

ring with our mirth.

* Poet Ireland.

Come Back To Erin

1. Come back to Erin, Mavourneen, Mavourneen,
   Come back Aroon, to the land of thy birth,
   Come with the shamrocks and springtime, Mavourneen,
   And it's Killarney shall ring with our mirth.
   Sure when we lent ye to beautiful England,
   Little we thought of the lone winter days,
   Little we thought of the hush of the starshine
   Over the mountain, the Bluffs and the Brays.
   Then come back to Erin, Mavourneen, Mavourneen,
   Come back again to the land of thy birth;
   Come back to Erin, Mavourneen, Mavourneen
   And it's Killarney shall ring with our mirth.

2. Over the green sea, Mavourneen, Mavourneen,
   Long shone the white sail that bore thee away,
   Riding the white waves that fair summer mornin',
   Just like a May flower afloat on the bay.
   O but my heart sank when clouds came between us,
   Like a grey curtain, the rain falling down,
   Hid from my sad eyes the path o'er the ocean
   Far, far away where my colleen had flown.
   Chorus ...

3. O, may the Angels, awakin' and sleepin',
   Watch o'er my bird in the land far away.
   And it's my prayers will consign to their keepin',
   Care o' my jewel by night and by day.
   When by the fireside I watch the bright embers,
   Then all my heart flies to England and thee,
   Cravin' to know if my darlin' remembers,
   Or if her thoughts may be crossin' to me.
Chorus ...

Daughters of Erin

Then re - mem-ber wher-ev-er your gob-let is crown'd Thro' this

world wheth-er east-ward or west-ward you roam, When a cup to the

smile of dear wom-an goes round, Oh! re - mem-ber the smile

which a - dorns her at home

* Poet Ireland.

Daughters Of Erin

Then remember wherever you goblet is crown'd
Thro' this world whether eastward or westward you roam,
When a cup to the smile of dear woman goes round,
Oh! remember the smile which adorns her at home

Dear Old Ireland

The po-ets sing of love and wine, Of her-oes liv-ing at their

shrine, The noblest theme of all is mine, To sing of dear old

Ire- land.   A song of E-rin's noble fame, Where despot's rule

could never tame, And ho-ly free-dom more than name, In loving

dear old Ire-land. Sing the cho-rus loud and free Till it rings

from sea to sea, Our toast ev-er-more will be A health to dear

old Ire-land.

Dear Old Ireland

1. The poets sing of love and wine,
   Of heroes living at their shrine,
   The noblest theme of all is mine,
   To sing of dear old Ireland.
   A song of Erin's noble fame,
   Where despot's rule could never tame,
   And holy freedom more than name,
Chorus
   In loving dear old Ireland.
   Sing the chorus loud and free
   Till it rings from sea to sea,
   Our toast evermore will be
   A health to dear old Ireland.

2. There's Moore whose lov'd immortal lays,
   Around the world the theme of praise,
   His genius shone to proudly raise
   The name of dear old Ireland.
   Lord Edward, Emmet, and Wolfe Tone,
   And thousands more, whose name unknown,
   Nor fear'd to die but proud to own
   Their love to dear old Ireland.
Chorus ...

3. The emigrant from Erin's shore
   Perhaps may never see her more,
   He loves to dream and ponder o'er
   The scenes in dear old Ireland.
   To scenes of love, and hope, and joy,
   To scenes of mirth without alloy,
   To scenes where greed could ne'er destroy
   The soul from dear old Ireland.
Chorus ...

Dublin Bay

He sail'd a-way in a gal-lant bark, Roy Neil and his fair young

bride He had ven-tur'd all, in that bounding oak, That dash'd

o'er the sil-ver tide But his heart was young and his spir-it

light and he dash'd the tear a-way As he watch'd the shores

re-cede from sight, Of his own sweet Dub-lin Bay.

142

Dublin Bay

1. He sail'd away in a gallant bark,
   Roy Neil and his fair young bride
   He had ventur'd all, in that bounding oak,
   That dash'd o'er the silver tide
   But his heart was young and his spirit light
   And he dash'd the tear away
   As he watch'd the shores recede from sight,
   Of his own sweet Dublin Bay.

2. Three days they sailed and a storm arose,
   And the light'ning swept the deep,
   And the thunder crash broke the short repose,
   Of the weary sea-boy's sleep.
   Roy Neill he clasp'd his weeping bride,
   And he kissed her tears away,
   "Oh love 'twas a fatal hour", she cried,
   "When we left sweet Dublin Bay."

3. On the crowded deck of the doomed ship,
   Some stood in their mute despair,
   And some, more calm, with a holy lip,
   Sought the God of the storm in pray'r.
   "She has struck on the rock", the sea-men cried
   In the breath of their wild dismay,
   And the ship went down, and the fair young bride
   That sail'd from Dublin Bay.

Homes of Donegal

I've just stepped in to see you all, I'll only stay a while   I want to see how you're gettin' on, I want to see you smile;   I'm happy to be back again, I greet you big and small   For there's no place else on earth just like The Homes of Don-e-gal.

Homes of Donegal

1. I've just stepped in to see you all,
   I'll only stay a while
   I want to see how you're gettin' on,
   I want to see you smile;
   I'm happy to be back again,
   I greet you big and small
   For there's no place else on earth just like
   The Homes of Donegal.

2. I always see the happy faces,
   Smiling at the door,
   The kettle swingin' on the crook
   As I step up the floor;
   And soon the taypot's fillin' up
   Me cup that's far from small.
   For your hearts are like your mountains
   In the Homes of Donegal.

3. To see your homes at parting day
   Of that I never tire
   And hear the porridge bubblin'
   In a big pot on the fire
   The lamp a-light, the dresser bright
   The big clock on the wall,
   O, a sight serene celestial scene
   In the Homes of Donegal.

4. I long to sit along with you
   And while away the night
   With tales of yore and fairy lore
   Beside your fires so bright
   And then to see prepared for me
   A shake-down by the wall
   There's repose for weary wand'rers
   In the Homes of Donegal.

5. Outside the night winds shriek and how!
   Inside there's peace and calm
   A picture on the wall up there's
   Our Saviour with a lamb
   The hope of wandering sheep like me
   And all who rise and fall
   There's a touch of heavenly love around
   The Homes of Donegal.

6. A tramp I am and a tramp I've been
   A tramp I'll always be
   Me father tramped, me mother tramped
   Sure trampin's bred in me
   If some there are my ways disdain
   And won't have me at all
   Sure I'll always find a welcome
   In the Homes of Donegal.

7. The time has come and I must go
   I bid you all adieu
   The open highway calls me forth
   To do the things I do
   And when I'm trampin' far away
   I'll hear your voices call
   And pleace God I'll soon return into
   The Homes of Donegal.

In County Clare

As I sit all a-lone in a land strange to me. My thoughts travel

back o'er the vast roll-ing sea. To the land that I love, to a

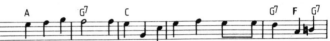

spot I call home. No oth-er ex-cels it, though the world I may

roam. Sure there ne-ver was an-o-ther land like Ire-land. It's

the dear-est land in all the world to me. For my heart is al-

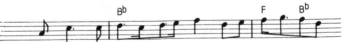

ways there! Way back in County Clare. In that lit- tle ca-bin

far a-cross the sea.

In County Clare

1. As I sit all alone in a land strange to me.
   My thoughts travel back o'er the vast rolling sea.
   To the land that I love, to a spot I call home.
   No other excels it, though the world I may roam.
Chorus
   Sure there never was another land like Ireland.
   It's the dearest land in all the world to me.
   For my heart is always there!
   Way back in County Clare.
   In that little cabin far across the sea.

2. You're the home of the dear little shamrock so green,
   Sure its no other place in the world to be seen.
   With its lakes of Killarney so lovely so grand.
   No wonder I love you, my own dear Ireland.
Chorus ...

Killarney

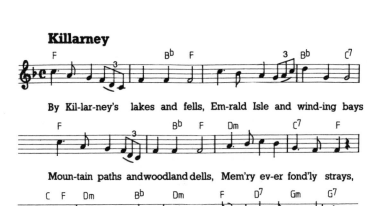

By Kil-lar-ney's lakes and fells, Em-rald Isle and wind-ing bays

Moun-tain paths and woodland dells, Mem'ry ev-er fond'ly strays,

Boun-teous nature loves all lands, Beau-ty wan-ders ev-'

ry-where Footprints leave on ma-ny strands But her home is

surely there. An-gels fold their wings and rest In that Eden

of the West; Beau-ty's home, Kil-lar-ney, Heav'ns reflex Kil-

lar-ney.

Killarney

1. By Killarney's lakes and fells,
   Emrald Isle and winding bays
   Mountain paths and woodland dells,
   Mem'ry ever fond'ly strays,
   Bounteous nature loves all lands,
   Beauty wanders ev'rywhere
   Footprints leave on many strands
   But her home is surely there.
   Angels fold their wings and rest
   In that Eden of the West;
   Beauty's home, Killarney,
   Heav'ns reflex Killarney.

2. No place else can charm the eye,
   With such bright and varied tints,
   Ev'ry rock that you pass by,
   Verdure broiders or besprints.
   Virgin there the green grass grows,
   Ev'ry morn Spring's natal day,
   Bright hued berries daff the snows,
   Smiling Winters' frown away!

   Angels often pausing there
   Doubt if Eden were more fair,
   Beauty's home, Killarney,
   Heav'ns reflex, Killarney.

My Wild Irish Rose

My wild I-rish Rose,   The sweet-est flow'r that grows,

You may search ev'ry-where but none can com-pare With my wild

I-rish Rose.   My wild I-rish Rose,   The dear-est flow'r that

grows   And some day for my sake, she may let me take The bloom

from my wild I-rish rose.

My Wild Irish Rose

My wild Irish Rose,
The sweetest flow'r that grows,
You may search ev'rywhere
But none can compare
With my wild Irish Rose.
My wild Irish Rose,
The dearest flow'r that grows
And some day for my sake,
She may let me take
The bloom from my wild Irish rose.

Oh! Erin* Dear.

Oh! E-rin dear, my thoughts are with the ev-er No other land

can stir my heart like thee Why did I from my friends and dear

ones sev-er To make my home so far a-cross the sea? I miss thy

jov -ial sons and winsome daugh-ters The songs of chil-dren on

the village green, I yearn to hear the sound of rushing wa-ters

And more than all I miss my faith-ful lass Ei-leen.

* Poet Ireland.

154

Oh! Erin Dear
(An Exile's Lament)

1. Oh! Erin dear, my thoughts are with the ever
   No other land can stir my heart like thee
   Why did I from my friends and dear ones sever
   To make my home so far across the sea?

   I miss thy jovial sons and winsome daughters
   The songs of children on the village green,
   I yearn to hear the sound of rushing waters
   And more than all I miss my faithful lass Eileen.

2. The strangers here are kind and noble hearted
   And sure, I blush to think of all their care,
   But thoughts will rise of those from whom I'm parted,
   That wake the sigh and haste the falling tear.
   I dream at night of sunset on the shingle,
   Of jaunting cars, and nestling shamrocks green,
   Och! then I wake, and all my senses tingle
   With memories of my home and you, my sweet Eileen.

Oh! Steer My Barque to Erin's* Isle

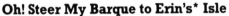

Oh! I have roam'd in many lands, And many friends I've met;   Not

one fair scene or kind-ly smile, Can this fond heart forget. But

I'll   confess that I'm content, No more I wish to roam, Oh! steer

my barque to E-rin's Isle, for E-rin is my home, Oh! steer my

barque to Erin's   Isle,   For Erin is my home.

* Poet Ireland

Oh! Steer My Barque To Erin's Isle

1. Oh! I have roam'd in many lands,
   And many friends I've met;
   Not one fair scene or kindly smile,
   Can this fond heart forget.
   But I'll confess that I'm content,
   No more I wish to roam,
   Oh! steer my barque to Erin's Isle,
   For Erin is my home,
   Oh! steer my barque to Erin's Isle,
   For Erin is my home.

2. If England were my place of birth,
   I'd love her tranquil shore,
   If Bonnie Scotland were my home,
   Her mountains I'd adore.
   Though pleasant days in both I pass,
   I dream of days to come.
   Oh! steer my barque to Erin's Isle,
   For Erin is my home,
   Oh! steer my barque to Erin's Isle,
   For Erin is my home.

Rosin The Bow

I was born in the county of Ker-ry near the town of sweet Ca-hir-ci-veen; Ah, it's there that the people are merry, 'mid the hills and the valleys so green My grandfather had an old fid-dle ah 'twas he made the melodies flow And al-ways my cra-dle was rock'd to the tune of rol-licking Rosin the Bow Then boys, take the floor with your colleens and shake up your heel and your toe Just loosen the fiddler's elbow, and he'll play you up Ros-in the Bow.

Rosin The Bow

1. I was born in the county of Kerry
   Near the town of sweet Cahirciveen;
   Ah, it's there that the people are merry,
   'Mid the hills and the valleys so green
   My grandfather had an old fiddle
   Ah 'twas he made the melodies flow
   And always my cradle was rock'd
   To the tune of rollicking Rosin the Bow
Chorus
   Then boys, take the floor with your colleens
   And shake up your heel and your toe
   Just loosen the fiddler's elbow,
   And he'll play you up Rosin the Bow.

2. The day I was married to Eileen
   My grandad was still to the fore,
   With his fiddle to set your heart dancing,
   When the brogues met the good earthen floor.
   Now I think of the bright smiling faces;
   Most are gone where the best of us go.
   Still in mem'ry I hear the glad laughter
   And the strains of sweet Rosin the Bow.
Chorus

3. When my troubles and trials are over,
   May my dust rest in Kerry's dear ground:
   And my soul that loved God and old Ireland,
   To Heaven I hope will be bound.
   And there, I feel sure I'll see round me,
   The dear ones I loved here below.
   On the harp I'm no good, but with cat-gut and wood,
   Sure I'll crack them up Rosin the Bow.
Chorus

Sprig of Shillelah

Och love is the soul of a nate I-rish man He loves all that's

lovely, loves all that he can, With his sprig of Shil-le-lah and

Shamrock so green With his sprig of Shillelah and Shamrock so

green, His heart is good humour'd, 'tis honest and sound, no

malice or hatred is there to be found; He courts and he marries

he drinks and he fights, For love, all for love, for in that he

delights, With his sprig of Shillelah, and Shamrock so green,

With his sprig of Shillelah and Shamrock so green.

160

Sprig of Shillelah

1. Och love is the soul of a nate Irish man
   He loves all that's lovely, loves all that he can,
   With his sprig of Shillelah and Shamrock so green
   With his sprig of Shillelah and Shamrock so green,
   His heart is good humour'd, 'tis honest and sound,
   No malice or hatred is there to be found;
   He courts and he marries, he drinks and he fights,
   For love, all for love, for in that he delights,
   With his sprig of Shillelah, and Shamrock so green,
   With his sprig of Shillelah and Shamrock so green.

2. Who e'er had the luck to see Donnybrook fair,
   An Irishman all in his glory was there,
   With his sprig of Shillelah, and Shamrock so green,
   With his sprig of Shillelah, and Shamrock so green.
   His clothes, spick and span, new without e'er a speck,
   A neat Barcelona tied round his nice neck,
   He goes to a tent, and he spends half a crown,
   He meets with a friend, and for love knocks him down,
   With his sprig of Shillelah, and Shamrock so green,
   With his sprig of Shillelah, and Shamrock so green.

3. At evening returning, as homeward he goes,
   His heart soft with whiskey, his head soft with blows,
   From a sprig of Shillelah, and Shamrock so green
   From a sprig of Shillelah, and Shamrock so green.
   He meets with his Shelah, who blushing a smile,
   Cries "Get ye gone Pat" yet consents all the while,
   To the Priest soon they go, and nine months after that
   A fine baby cries "How do you do father Pat"
   With your sprig of Shillelah, and Shamrock so green
   With your sprig of Shillelah, and Shamrock so green.

St. Patrick's Day

Tho' dark are our sorrows, today we'll forget them, And smile

thru' our tears like a sunbeam in show'rs; There never were hearts,

our rulers would let them, More form'd to be grateful and

blest than ours! But just when the chain Has ceased to pain, And

hope has enwreath'd it 'round with flow'rs, There comes a new

link, Our spirit to sink! Oh, the joy that we taste, like the

light of the poles, Is a flash amid darkness too brilliant to

stay; But tho't were the last little spark in our souls, We must

light it up now, on our Prin-ce's Day.

St. Patrick's Day

Tho' dark are our sorrows, today we'll forget them,
And smile thru' our tears like a sunbeam in show'rs;
There never were hearts, if our rulers would let them,
More form'd to be grateful and blest than ours!
But just when the chain has ceased to pain,
And hope has enwreath'd it 'round with flow'rs,
There comes a new link,
Our spirit to sink!
Oh, the joy that we taste, like the light of the poles,
Is a flash amid darkness too brilliant to stay;
But tho't were the last little spark in our souls,
We must light it up now, on our Price's Day.

That's An Irish Lullaby

Too - ra - loo - ra - loo - ral,   Too - ra - loo - ra - li,

Too - ra - loo - ra - loo -ral,   Hush now don't you cry!

Too - ra - loo - ra - loo - ral,   Too - ra - loo - ra -li,

Too - ra - loo - ra - loo - ral,   That's an I - rish lul-la-

by.

That's An Irish Lullaby

Tooralooralooral, tooralooralooral, tooralooralooral,
Hush now don't you cry!
Tooralooralooral, tooralooralooral, tooralooralooral,
That's an Irish lullaby.

Words spoken:
Over in Killarney, many years ago,
My mother sang a song to me
In tones so soft and low;
And I'd give the world
If I could her sing that song today:

The Dear Little Shamrock

There's a dear lit-tle plant that grows in our Isle 'Twas St.

Patrick him-self sure that set it: And the sun on his la-bour

with pleas-ure did smile, And with dew from his eye often wet it

It shines thro' the bog, thro' the brake, thro' the mire-land

And he call'd it the dear lit-tle shamrock of Ire-land. The dear

lit tle Shamrock, the sweet little Shamrock, the dear little,

sweet lit- tle Shamrock'of Ire-land.

The Dear Little Shamrock

1. There's a dear little plant that grows in our Isle
   'Twas St. Patrick himself sure that set it:
   And the sun on his labour with pleasure did smile,
   And with dew from his eye often wet it
   It shines thro'the bog, thro'the brake, thro'the mireland
   And he call'd it the dear little shamrock of Ireland.
Chorus
   The dear little Shamrock, the sweet little Shamrock,
   The dear little, sweet little Shamrock of Ireland.

2. The dear little plant still grows in our Isle,
   Fresh and fair as the daughters of Erin,
   Whose smile can bewitch and whose eyes can beguile,
   In each climate they ever appear in.
   For they shine through the bog, through the brake,
   and the mireland,
   Just like their own dear little Shamrock of Ireland.
Chorus ...

3. The dear little plant that springs from our soil,
   When its three little leaves are extended,
   Denotes from its stalk we together should toil,
   And ourselves by ourselves be befriended.
   And still through the bog, through the brake, and the mireland,
   From one root should branch like the Shamrock of Ireland.
Chorus ...

The Kerry Dance

O the days of the Ker-ry danc-ing, O the ring of the pi-per's

tune! O for one of those hours of gladness, Gone a-las! like our

youth, too soon. When the boys be-gan to gather in the glen, of

a summer night, And the Kerry piper's tuning made us long with

wild delight. O to think of it, O to dream of it, Fills my heart

with tears!

The Kerry Dance

O the days of the Kerry dancing,
O the ring of the piper's tune!
O for one of those hours of gladness,
Gone alas! like our youth, too soon.
When the boys began to gather in the glen, of a summer night,
And the Kerry piper's tuning made us long with wild delight.
O to think of it, O to dream of it,
Fills my heart with tears!

The Meeting of the Waters

There is not in the wide world a valley so sweet, As the vale in

whose bosom the bright wa-ters meet, Oh! the last rays of feel-

ing and life must de-part, Ere the bloom of that val-ley shall

fade from my heart, Ere the bloom of that valley shall fade from

my heart.

The Meeting of the Waters

1. There is not in the wide world a valley so sweet,
   As the vale in whose bosom the bright waters meet,
   Oh! the last rays of feeling and life must depart,
   Ere the bloom of that valley shall fade from my heart,
   Ere the bloom of that valley shall fade from my heart.

2. Yet it was not that nature had shed o'er the scene
   Her purest of crystal, and brightest of green,
   'Twas not her soft magic, of streamlet or hill,
   Oh no, it was something, more exquisite still,
   Oh no, it was something, more exquisite still.

3. 'Twas that friends, the belov'd of my bosom were near,
   Who made every dear scene of enchantment more dear,
   And who felt how the best chains of nature improve,
   When we see them reflected from looks that we love,
   When we see them reflected from looks that we love.

4. Sweet vale of Avoca, how calm could I rest,
   In thy bosom of shade, with the friends I love best,
   Where the storms that we feel, in this cold world should cease
   And our hearts like thy waters, be mingled in peace.
   And our hearts like thy waters, be mingled in peace.

There's A Heart In Old Ireland

Oh! the day bright and clear, and the sky deepest blue, And my

thoughts turn back to a heart fond and true There's a dear lit-

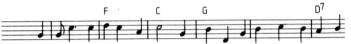

tle cabin far o-ver the sea Where someone is an-xious-ly waiting

for me. There's a heart in old Ireland that's pin-ing for me,

And there's „Two I-rish Eyes", that gaze out on the sea, But I'll

soon be re-turning and once a-gain be, With the heart in old

Ireland   that's pin-ing for me.

172

There's A Heart In Old Ireland

1. Oh! the day bright and clear, and the sky deepest blue,
   And my thoughts turn back to a heart fond and true
   There's a dear little cabin far over the sea
   Where someone is anxiously waiting for me.
Chorus
   There's a heart in old Ireland that's pining for me,
   And there's „Two Irish Eyes", that gaze out on the sea,
   But I'll soon be returning and once again be,
   With the heart in old Ireland that's pining for me.

2. Oh! in fancy I see my old Ireland so dear,
   And the Lakes of Killarney so lovely and clear,
   I can see the old Shannon flow down to the sea,
   Where I first met the heart that is pining for me.
Chorus ...

The Rose of Aranmore

My thoughts to-day though I'm far

a-way   dwell on Tyr-conn-ell's shore.   The salt sea air and

the coll-eens fair   of love-ly green Gwee-dore   There's a

flow-er there be-yound com-pare that I'll   treas-ure ev-er-more.

That grand coll-een in her gown of green she's the rose of

Ar-an-more.

The Rose of Aranmore

1. My thoughts today though I'm far away dwell on Tyrconnell's shore.
   The salt sea air and the colleens fair of lovely green Gweedore
   There's a flower there beyound compare that I'll treasure evermore.
   That grand colleen in her gown of green
   She's the rose of Aranmore.

2. I've travelled far'neath the northern star the day I said good-bye,
   And seen many maids in the golden glades beneath a tropic sky.
   There's a vision in my reverie I always will adore:
   That grand colleen in her gown of green –
   She's the rose of Aranmore.

3. But soon I will return again to the scenes I loved so well,
   Where many an Irish lad and lass their tales of love to tell.
   The silvery dunes and blue lagoons, along the Rosses shore,
   And that green colleen in her gown of green –
   She's the rose of Aranmore.

Song titles

Index of first lines